THE ACT OF BIBLE READING

A Multidisciplinary Approach to Biblical Interpretation

GORDON D. FEE

CRAIG M. GAY

JAMES HOUSTON

J. I. PACKER

EUGENE PETERSON

LOREN WILKINSON

edited by

ELMER DYCK

InterVarsity Press
Downers Grove, Illinois

InterVarsity Press® is the book-publishing division of InterVarsity Christian Fellowship®, a student movement active on campus at hundreds of universities, colleges and schools of nursing in the United States of America, and a member movement of the International Fellowship of Evangelical Students. For information about local and regional activities, write Public Relations Dept., InterVarsity Christian Fellowship, 6400 Schroeder Rd., P.O. Box 7895, Madison, WI 53707-7895.

Scripture quotations, unless otherwise indicated, are the contributors' own translations.

Cover illustration: Scala/Art Resource, NY: Campin, Robert. Saint Barbara. *Prado, Madrid, Spain.*

ISBN 0-8308-1623-2

Printed in the United States of America ∞

Library of Congress Cataloging-in-Publication Data

The act of Bible reading: a multidisciplinary approach to biblical
  interpretation/Elmer Dyck, ed.
     p.   cm.
  Includes bibliographical references.
  ISBN 0-8308-1623-2 (pbk.: alk. paper)
  1. Bible—Hermeneutics. 2. Bible—Reading. I. Dyck, Elmer,
1947- .
  BS476.A315   1996
  220.6'01—dc20   *95-48966*
                                                        CIP

16	15	14	13	12	11	10	9	8	7	6	5	4	3	2	1
09	08	07	06	05	04	03	02	01	00	99	98	97	96		

Foreword: *Caveat Lector/Eugene Peterson* _____ 7

1 History as Context for Interpretation/*Gordon D. Fee* _____ 10

2 Canon as Context for Interpretation/*Elmer Dyck* _____ 33

3 Theology & Bible Reading/*J. I. Packer* _____ 65

4 The Sociology of Knowledge & the Art of Suspicion
  (A Sociological Interpretation of Interpretation)/*Craig M. Gay* _____ 88

5 Hermeneutics & the Postmodern Reaction Against
  "Truth"/*Loren Wilkinson* _____ 114

6 Toward a Biblical Spirituality/*James M. Houston* _____ 148

Notes _____ 174

Foreword
Caveat Lector

Eugene Peterson

For Christians, the reading and study of holy Scripture as our authority in all matters of faith and practice is a core activity, not an add-on. But in our contemporary world, with its proliferating fashions in "spirituality," more and more people are choosing other authorities and guides to salvation. As up-to-date and attractive as many of these options may appear, we Christians say no to them.

We say no to working ourselves up into visionary states of ecstasy in order to get in touch with God. We say no to undertaking Herculean tasks of moral heroism in order to discover the divine potentialities within us. We say no to going off to a mountain cave and emptying ourselves of all thought and feeling and desire so that there is nothing to keep us from immediate access to Reality. We Christians are sometimes impressed by these spiritual pyrotechnics and on occasion even "ooh and ah" over them. But our wiser guides do not encourage us to pursue them. In contrast to the glamorous spiritualities, ours is a pedestrian way, literally: putting one foot in front of the other as we follow Jesus. In order to know who he is, where he is going and how to walk in his steps, we reach for a book, *the* book, and read it: holy Scripture.

Historically Christians have been as concerned about *how* we read the Bible as *that* we read it. The Christian community as a whole has never assumed that it is sufficient to place a Bible in a person's hands with a command to read it. That would be as foolish as handing a set of car keys to an adolescent, giving her a Honda and saying, "Drive it." And just as dangerous. The danger is that in having our hands on a piece of technology, we impose our ignorant or destructive will upon it.

For print is technology. We have God's Word in our hands, *our hands.* We can now handle it. It is easy enough to suppose that we are in control of it, that we can manage it, that we can use it and apply it.

There is more to the Honda than the technology of mechanics. And there is more to the Bible than the technology of print. Surrounding the machine technology of the Honda there is a world of gravity and inertia, values and velocity, surfaces and obstructions, Chevrolets and Fords, traffic regulations and the police, other drivers, snow and ice and rain. There is far more to a car than its gearshift and steering wheel. There is far more to driving a car than turning a key in the ignition and stepping on the accelerator. Those who don't know that are soon dead or maimed.

And those who don't know the *world* of the Bible are likewise dangerous to themselves and others. So as we hand out Bibles and urge people to read them, we also say, "*Caveat lector*—let the reader beware."

Men and women shopping in the marketplace for vegetables and meat, carpets and skirts, horses and automobiles, are warned by their experienced parents and grandparents, "*Caveat emptor:* let the buyer beware." The market is not what it seems. More is going on than a simple exchange of goods. Sellers and buyers don't operate out of the same mindset. Their intentions are seldom identical. Let the buyer beware.

And let the reader beware. Just having print on the page and knowing how to distinguish nouns from verbs is not enough. Reading the Bible can get you into a lot of trouble. Few things are more important in the Christian community than reading the Scriptures *rightly.* The holy Scriptures carry immense authority. Read wrongly, they can ignite war, legitimize abuse, sanction hate, cultivate arrogance. Not only can, but have . . . *do.* This is present danger.

So *caveat lector*—let the reader beware. Read, but read rightly. The adverb *rightly* in this context does not only mean accurately; it means right-heartedly as well as right-mindedly, what the biblical writers referred to as uprightly.

Read the Scriptures, not to learn something that will give us an advantage over our nonreading neighbors or an occasional emotional uplift, but in order to live to the glory of God.

It is essential that we round up all the help available in the acquisition of Scripture-reading skills, skills that orient us in the mind and heart of the Bible as well as the words of the Bible, skills that integrate keen minds and devout hearts, that insist that there is no understanding of Scripture that is not at the same time a living of it, that have no interest in exegesis that is not simultaneously holy obedience.

The essays in this volume represent some of the best help available to those who wish to acquire Scripture-reading skills. The writers of these essays, working together in the community of prayer and learning that is Regent College, are masters at this. Not only do they love Scripture and live it, but they are wise and accurate guides ready to help the rest of us as we pursue our lifelong quest to understand and live what we read in our Bibles.

1

History
as Context
for Interpretation

Gordon D. Fee

I T WAS MANY YEARS ago now. I was home in bed on a Sunday morning, sick as a dog. Unable to attend church, I decided to do the next best thing—listen to a church service on radio station WMBI in Chicago. A very well-known preacher was expounding 1 Corinthians 3:16-17. He was impassioned and eloquent, but he had the text wrong. The temple, he was telling his live and radio audience, referred to the individual believer, especially to her or his body. And we had better be holy, he exhorted, or God would destroy us. I turned off the radio and did not get better.

The next year, same place, same station, a different but equally well-known preacher was expounding 1 Corinthians 3:10-15. He also applied his passage to the individual Christian, to how we build our lives on the foundation of Christ. Although he said much that was fine and true, he did not in fact address what Paul was talking about in this passage.

If this is how well-known preachers handle the biblical text, I asked myself, what hope is there for the ordinary believer, who has very little time for study and is being told that texts mean something quite foreign to what Paul himself was saying to the Corinthians? How many of God's good people, far from celebrating the Lord's Supper as they should, have had 1 Corinthians 11:29 (in the KJV) laid on them so that the communion table was a time of deep introspection, solemnity, and heavy guilt!

All of these interpretations fail to take history seriously as the proper first context for interpretation. From the perspective of the biblical scholar, the first step toward valid interpretation of Scripture is a historical investigation known as *exegesis,* which means the determination of the originally intended meaning of a text. "History as context for interpretation" does not refer to our own history, but to the original setting(s) of the biblical texts themselves. The task of interpretation is nothing less than to bridge the historical—and therefore cultural—gap between them and us. We thereby determine both what and how God spoke to them and how that same word speaks to us as an eternal word.

It is precisely because our own histories, both personal and cultural, are so different from those of the writers of sacred Scripture that we must engage in the interpretative process called *hermeneutics,* which refers to the whole task of interpretation, including exegesis and the correlation and application of exegesis to theological thinking and Christian life.

To the biblical scholar hermeneutics means that kind of interpretation that views Scripture as divine revelation, which is therefore the basis for Christian theology, life and behavior. Thought of in these terms, hermeneutics seeks that "plain sense" of Scripture, inspired by the Spirit and understood with the help of the Spirit, which is equally applicable and obligatory as God's word for all people at all times in all settings.

This is not to deprecate the kind of devotional Bible reading that most people do. Reading with open heart and mind, they trust the Holy Spirit to speak directly from the text of Scripture into their own lives. Someone who is experiencing personal difficulty might be reading from Isaiah 45 and hear in a personal sense God's promise to Israel (to bring them back from captivity): "I will go before you and will level the mountains." Such experiences are common to most people who read the Bible prayerfully and lie within the inherent power of Scripture.

Because such moments are very personal, no one would reasonably contend that this *meaning* of the text is universally applicable to all other believers, even though one might share with others such experiences from God's living word. But the *study* of Scripture, whereby God's people grow in understanding and more into the likeness of Christ, requires us to engage in the historical exercise called exegesis.

The Need

The need for good exegesis can first of all be illustrated by scores of examples like those noted above that result from reading biblical texts in light of our own experience, culture, theological bias or simply misinformation.

But the need also arises from much more significant factors than inadequate or simply bad interpretation. Essentially the need is the result of two realities: (1) a reader is by that very fact also an interpreter of what she or he reads; and (2) the nature of Scripture.

First, it is simply not possible to read Scripture without interpreting as we read. Anyone dependent on an English translation for reading the Bible is already dependent on the interpretation of the translators. That translators must also interpret gives rise to the many differences among translations. Note, for example, two different renderings of 1 Corinthians 7:21. The NIV reads, "Were you a slave when you were called? Don't let it trouble you—although if you can gain your freedom, do so." Goodspeed *(An American Translation),* who is followed by a large number of New Testament scholars, understands the text to say exactly the opposite: "But even if you can gain your freedom, make the most of your present condition instead." Both translations are based on the same Greek text!

But translators are not to blame for the fact that readers also interpret what they read. Readers bring a whole bag full of cultural and lexical assumptions to the text, often unaware that they are doing so. Ask yourself, for example, how you respond to the following three translations of Paul's second question in 1 Corinthians 1:20: "Where is the scribe?" (KJV); "Where is the scholar?" (NIV); "Where is the expert in the law?" (Bauer's lexicon). Paul is rhetorically challenging the Jewish rabbi, the expert in Jewish law. The person with some biblical background may catch that from the KJV or Bauer, but the untrained reader may miss Paul's point altogether because each translation could mean something quite different to her or him.

Thus the first reason we must learn to do exegesis is that as readers we are already interpreters of Scripture, whether we realize it or not. The real question is whether we do it *well.*

The second reason one must learn to do exegesis and learn to do it well, has to do with our conviction as to the nature of Scripture. By definition, Christians believe—at least historical orthodoxy believes—that the Bible is the Word of God given in human words in history. That is, as we believe about our Savior, so too we believe about Scripture that it is at once both human and divine. Because it is divine, because we believe it is God's word, it is incumbent on us to know what it means and to obey. But because God's eternal word was given in human words in history, those words were themselves conditioned by the culture, background and speech patterns of the author. God's eternal word was spoken in historically particular moments.

We would not have it otherwise. The Book of Mormon was allegedly written on golden tablets in a nonexistent language (Smith's alphabetic hieroglyph is quite impossible), requiring magical glasses to be translated into Elizabethan English with over a thousand grammatical errors. Rather too conveniently, the tablets were carted off by an angel so that no human eye could see or investigate them. Such a magical book could scarcely have come from the eternal God who has revealed himself in our human history, both in Scripture and in the person of his Son. To the contrary, our .book lives and breathes real human history—and is open to investigation by all.

But precisely because the Bible, inspired by God the Holy Spirit himself, also breathes real humanity, we must learn to interpret it. Because its human authors spoke their own language, out of their own culture and in their own history, we must go back to them and listen to what they meant within their own historical contexts if we are going to hear the word of the living God—both to them and to us. Precisely because God spoke his eternal word to them within their own particular history, we can take great confidence that he will speak again and again out of that context into lives all over the globe.

Our Predecessors
It has sometimes been argued that such a view of exegesis is very modern, and therefore not all people at all times in the past could have participated in such an interpretation of the biblical text. But that is an inadequate reading of the history of interpretation.

It is true that over the past two hundred years we have had better access to the historical tools that very often enable us to get closer to the author's original intent. It is also true that the "plain meaning of the text" has been a part of biblical interpretation throughout the history of the church. This is more especially true of the so-called Antiochene school (including such giants as the sainted John Chrysostom [d. 407] and Theodore of Mopsuestia [d. 428]) and the Reformation, especially the expositions of John Calvin.

On the other hand, it was also one way of interpreting the text (along with its spiritual, analogical or allegorical sense), even if not the more important one, articulated in the so-called Alexandrian school by its quintessential interpreter, Origen (d. 254). It was not that Origen neglected or ran roughshod over the meaning of the text in its historical context; he showed himself quite expert at such when it suited his purposes. Origen—and much of the later church that followed him—held that every word and every detail of Scripture should have "meaning" for the believer. Hence he and they had a field day with such things as parables. They learned to treat historical narratives in the same way, as though they were parables. Otherwise the narrative is simply prosaic past tense with much that was either irrelevant or (especially in the Old Testament) filled with embarrassing details. Thus, Origen tells us, Jesus went down to Capernaum (Jn 2:12), meaning "field of consolation," because after the feasting at Cana and the incident of the wine, he needed to console both his own soul and those of his disciples.

The great difference between the earlier church and us, therefore, is not that we have discovered history whereas they did not. Rather, (1) they were far more willing than we are to find other ("deeper" or "hidden" meanings) in the text when the "plain meaning" did not suit them; (2) we insist that the universally applicable meaning of the text is related primarily to its originally intended meaning; and (3) we have greater advantages than they in terms of access to tools and resources to do this task.

The Method
The components of good exegesis are *context* and *content*.

The questions of context, the *why* questions, are in three parts. First there is the matter of *genre*—that is, what kind of literature am I interpreting? It makes a considerable difference in terms of original intent to know whether one is reading narrative, poetry, prophecy, apocalypse or letter. Each of these has its own special "rules" as to how and why it is put together.

Second, one must determine the *historical context*—that is, the historical setting of a given document. This includes both the historical-cultural setting in general (e.g., the nature of the city of Corinth and its people) as well as the particular historical situation to which Paul is speaking. We must ask, How are we to view the letter as a whole? The key is to ask further, What was going on in the Corinthian church and what is the present status of their relationship to Paul?

Third, for every word and sentence one must also be alert to the *literary context,* which has to do with the meaning of the passage in relationship to the sentences and paragraphs that immediately surround it. What does this passage mean in this context? Why has Paul said this at this point in his argument? Why does the psalmist include these words of lament or this cry for justice precisely at this point in his prayer or praise?

The content questions are basically the *what* questions. They have to do with the details of the text and include such matters as the original text (what words did Paul actually write in his letter?), lexicography (what do those words mean in their present context?), grammar (how do these words stand in relationship to one another?), and historical background (what kinds of historical allusions or presuppositions lie behind these words?).

Thus exegesis, the historical investigation into an author's original intent, may be outlined as follows:

I. Questions of context
   A. Genre
   B. Historical context
      1. General
      2. Specific
   C. Literary context
II. Questions of content
   A. Original text
   B. Meaning of words
   C. Grammar
   D. Historical background

With practice one may learn to answer the questions of context quite well. A knowledge of the original languages, however, is needed to answer many of the content questions, and one must learn to consult higher level sources that know the languages.

The Practice

In order to see how this all works out, and as an illustration both of need and practice, we will work through the process for 1 Corinthians, finally examining in some detail two passages in particular: 3:10-17 and 11:17-34 (especially v. 29).

Genre. Unfortunately, our Bibles have been formatted into verses, with every verse being its own paragraph. One result of this convention has been to give people the sense that all verses can stand on their own—very much as individual proverbs. Every verse is its own revelation of truth, quite apart from its context and the intent of the inspired author. This is especially significant for the matter of genre, where the sense of narrative or poetry, for example, has been quite destroyed by the versification.

There is a world of difference between poetry and prose, between narrative and imperative, between apocalypse and apothegm, between a hymn addressed to God and a prophetic oracle addressed to his people. One simply should not treat the anguish of personal lament as though God were speaking, revealing eternal theological truths. On this matter see especially Gordon D. Fee and Douglas Stuart, *How to Read the Bible for All Its Worth,* both for an understanding of the *nature* of the various biblical genres and for some guidelines for interpretation that apply to each in particular.

For reading the New Testament epistles, hence 1 Corinthians, the first crucial matter to note is that they are letters. As with most letters, they contain rather straightforward prose statements (although filled with metaphors and at times quoting or adapting other materials). Second, they are ad hoc documents (i.e., they were occasioned by some specific circumstance, either from the author's or recipient's side). It is their ad hoc, occasional nature that creates some of our difficulties in understanding because the author often assumes so much between himself and his readers. The more he assumes, the more difficult it is for us to be certain as to the specific historical situation.

In 1 Corinthians the letter was occasioned both by some oral reports (see 1:11; 5:1; 11:18) and by a letter from the Corinthian believers to Paul (7:1). From this exchange we learn a little about the situation because Paul needs to tell them what he has heard, so we also get in on it. He quotes from their letter (7:1; 8:1, 4), and so we can get some insights here as well. But all of this leads us to our next step in the process.

Historical context (in general). Here we need to know as much as we can about the Greco-Roman world, and as much as we can about the city of Corinth and its people. It will make a difference in our understanding of this letter to know that the Roman city of Corinth was just under one hundred years old when Paul arrived in it, that within that time it had become the third city of the empire, that it was known by ancients as "wealthy Corinth" because it controlled commerce going east and west, that it was a very cosmopolitan city with inhabitants from all over the empire, and that it was at once very religious and very sinful. Extremes of wealth and poverty lived sided by side.

The believing community included the full measure of this culture. In 1 Corinthians 6:9-11 Paul says that "such were some of you," following a rather graphic list of ten vices; in 12:13 he notes that the "one body of Christ" (in Corinth is implied) was composed of "Jew and Gentile, slave and free." First Corinthians 11:17-34 reveals tensions between rich and poor. These realities, especially the fact that the believers were mostly Gentiles (see 12:2), will affect our understanding of numerous passages. For example, it is often suggested that the problem of "idol food" in chapters 8—10 reflects a Gentile abuse of Jewish sensibilities about eating such food that was sold in the marketplace. But that interpretation will scarcely do, since Paul specifically says in 8:7 that the person with the weak conscience who is being injured by the "one with knowledge" (he does not in fact contrast "weak" with "strong") is a former idolater; and the problem in 8:10 is specifically that of eating this food in pagan temples, which would not have been a temptation for a Jewish believer.

Historical context (specific). This is the more crucial aspect of historical context, having to do with both the historical situation in Corinth that occasioned Paul's letter, as well as the relationship between Paul and this congregation. The significance of finding an adequate answer to this question cannot be overstated. On the one hand, failure to do so at all will cause us to read the letter in light of our own historical contexts. On the other hand, failure to do so adequately will cause us to miss some very important insights that are essential to a proper understanding of any number of texts. An improper view of the historical context may lead us considerably astray in our interpretation of many passages. For example, despite the frequency with which it has been repeated, there is not a shred of historical evidence for prostitutes having shaved heads. One will simply have to do better than that when reading 1 Corinthians 11:2-16.

Our letter serves as a good case in point. Because it was doubly occasioned, by the reports and by their letter, the traditional approach has been to view it as a letter in which Paul is *correcting* them in areas where they have gone astray and *informing* them in areas where they have asked his guidance. But such a view does not seem adequately to take into account several data from the letter, including the fierce defense of his apostleship and lifestyle in chapters 4 and 9 (cf. 14:36-38) and the generally combative nature of so much of the letter.

Several pieces of data from the letter itself will help us reconstruct its historical context more plausibly. First, there can be no question that some kind of "division" or "strife" existed within the community, and that the strife was being carried on in the name of "wisdom" with their former leaders as rallying points (1:10—3:23 makes this clear). However, it is difficult to know what to make of this matter for the rest of the letter. Nothing explicitly indicates that this internal strife was over theological or behavioral matters, or that they were deeply divided on *issues* as such. This is especially so in chapters 1—4, where the matter of "division" is addressed, but it is equally true for the rest of the letter. Moreover, the attempt to identify some of the later elements in the letter with the names of the teachers mentioned in 1:12 meets with very little success. We have just noted, for example, how this scarcely works in chapters 8—10 with the so-called Cephas (or Peter) party, since there is nothing Jewish in that controversy at all. Finally, it should also be noted that the letter in its entirety is addressed to the whole church, with no hint that he is speaking now to one group, then to another. If Paul were settling differences among them, one would expect at least some word to that effect; but in fact there is none. This leads us to note two other matters.

1. That some bad blood exists between the Corinthian church and Paul can scarcely be doubted. It erupted rather fully between the time of this letter and the following one (see 2 Cor 1:23—2:4; 7:2-16; 10:1—13:10); there is good evidence that it already existed by the time of our letter. Thus the very slogans, I am of Apollos, I am of Peter, imply that they are against Paul. In chapters 4 and 9 Paul explicitly defends himself against some who are "examining" him, or making him defend himself against their accusations (cf. 1 Cor 4:3-5; 9:3). Then there is the combative nature of so much of the letter. Rarely, if ever, does he merely inform; instead he attacks and challenges with all the weapons in his literary arsenal to convince them that he is right and they are wrong on these matters.

2. First Corinthians is the third piece of correspondence between Paul and this church. According to 5:9-11, Paul had written a previous letter, no longer extant, in which he told them to dissociate from people (intending brothers and sisters) who continued to practice sexual immorality, greed and idolatry. Most people tend to assume that his first letter to them and theirs to him are unrelated, passing in the mails as it were. But since there was no mail service in the empire (letters were sent with someone), it is far more likely historically that these three letters represent an exchange of correspondence: Paul to them; their response to Paul; Paul's response to their response (our 1 Corinthians).

This explains why, for example, Paul speaks to some of the same issues again in our letter—not because they have misunderstood Paul's prior instructions, but because they have disregarded them. Far from being a polite request for Paul's directions, their letter is in effect a response in which they are giving *reasons* for their disregard of his prohibitions. That they *could* do so is explained in part because some among them are calling Paul's authority into question; that they *did* do so is precisely what makes sense of the extremely rhetorical and combative nature of Paul's reply.

Although we cannot be absolutely certain as to the points of contention between them, the evidence of our letter is that they were calling both his apostleship and his gospel into question; and in every instance they seem to be modifying it toward Hellenism, toward their pagan past and Greek way of thinking.

Basically the Corinthian problem seems to be one of a false spirituality, in which they stand over against Paul as to what it means to be people of the Spirit. Their view of spirituality was highly individualistic, nonmaterialistic (i.e., the denial of the physical side of present existence; hence their denial of a future bodily resurrection), and enthusiastic, in which they had come to view the gift of tongues as evidence that they had already attained the spiritual life of the future. Because they spoke the "tongues of angels" (i.e., the language of heaven), they considered themselves already to have attained fullness of spirituality. They simply awaited the shucking off of the body in death, so that their spirituality could be complete. Such a view made them triumphalists (there was no place for the cross or weakness in such a view) who considered themselves already as the angels. Thus some were denying sexual relations within marriage, and by throwing off the customary head coverings they were obliterating sexual distinctions in the present age. For Paul all of this ultimately denies the gospel with its focus on Christ crucified and on the Spirit as enabling one to live in the present simultaneously in weakness and power.

We turn now to see how this understanding of the history affects our understanding of the texts themselves.

Literary context. This is what most people mean when they say, "Yes, but keep the text in its context." And they are right. It is a simple fact of writing that authors are intentional. They intend one thing by their words, and not several things, or anything that a reader might wish. This is not to say that authors are always clear or unambiguous. In 1 Corinthians 5:9-11 Paul had to correct the Corinthians' misreading of his earlier letter to them. But the very fact that he tries to correct their misreading is the clear evidence that he *intended* them to read it in one way and not in another.

The basic rule for understanding a biblical author is one that we would apply to any such writing as long as we keep the genre in view, of course, since the very choice of a genre in which to write says something about an author's intent. The rule: Words have meaning only in sentences; sentences have meaning only in relationship to other sentences in a paragraph (or some other unit of thought); and paragraphs have meaning in relationship to other paragraphs.

The question of literary context is singular and crucial: *What's the point?* Not only do we want to know *what* is said, but we want to know *why.* Why has Paul said these words at this point in his argument? In light of what has just been said, what is the point of saying *this?* And how does this lead into what is going to be said next? These are the crucial questions. Until they are answered satisfactorily, exegesis has not been completed.

Let us apply these questions to our two paragraphs (3:10-15 and 3:16-17), by which we can illustrate how both the historical and literary contexts converge to give us Paul's intent, which is thus the Holy Spirit's intent, and thus the word of God for us today. These texts have a long history of being misunderstood and therefore misapplied in the church. The reasons for the misunderstanding are certainly explicable. Paul's argument up to this point is not always immediately visible. Twentieth-century Christians tend to individualize texts and make them personally applicable whatever their original context. But to individualize *these* texts is to do them in and to miss hearing a very important word from God, which is nowhere else expressed with the kind of power and warning that one finds here.

Let us begin with the historical context noted above, that the letter is a response both to a letter and reports from Corinth which indicate that the church has taken a considerably anti-Pauline stance on many issues. This tension emerges especially in the problem that is spelled out in 1:10-17 and in Paul's response to it in the strong, rhetorical defense of chapter 4. The specific issue is some internal strife, with their various former teachers as the points of reference. But clearly their internal divisions are a symptom of a much deeper problem. The long argument over wisdom, human and divine, in 1:18—2:16 makes it clear that this strife is being carried on in the name of wisdom itself, which in this case must be something close to a technical term for Greek philosophy and rhetoric. A careful reading of chapter 4 indicates that whatever it meant for them to be enamored with wisdom, it concomitantly meant a rejection of Paul and his apostleship. But for Paul the matter was even worse. To carry on strife in the name of wisdom meant that the gospel itself was at stake. They were acting as if the gospel were merely another expression of this wisdom, and they were evaluating Paul and his gospel from this merely human point of view. Paul's response to all of this is our chapters 1—4.

From Paul's perspective three things need to be squared away: (1) Their quarrels in the name of wisdom indicated to Paul that they had radically misunderstood the basic nature of the gospel with its message of Christ crucified as God's way of bringing redemption to fallen humankind. (2) Strife in the name of their former leaders indicated that they also had a radical misunderstanding of the church and its leadership. To say "I am of Apollos" is to make Apollos the basis of the Christian community rather than Christ himself. (3) Deeply involved in this strife was their rejection of Paul and his apostleship, noted above.

A careful reading of chapters 1—4 will reveal that these are the three issues Paul takes up, and in this order. Thus 1:18—2:16 is his response to their radical misunderstanding of the nature of the gospel. After the transitional paragraph in 3:1-4, which is full of bite, he takes up their radical misunderstanding of the nature of church leadership in 3:5-15, and of the church itself in 3:16-17. Both of these issues are brought to a resounding conclusion in 3:18-23. But there remains the problem of their rejection of him and his apostleship, which is addressed in chapter 4.

Our present concern is with their misunderstanding of the church and its leadership. In order to understand this, we need a good sense of the argument to this point. Their quarrels over their leaders originate in their failure to grasp fully the nature of the gospel. Thus Paul begins by attacking the heart of their new fascination, wisdom itself. In a series of three paragraphs (1:18-25; 1:26-31; 2:1-5), he tries to get them to see that their own existence as Christians, especially in regard to their Christian beginnings, stands in total contradiction to their present "boasting" in men in the name of wisdom. Each paragraph is predicated on the same reality—namely, that the cross is not something to which one may add human wisdom and thereby make it superior; rather, the cross stands in absolute, uncompromising contradiction to human wisdom. The cross in fact is folly to wisdom humanly conceived; but it is *God's* folly, folly that is at the same time his wisdom and power.

Thus, up to 2:5 Paul is especially hard on wisdom humanly conceived. But he *has* urged that the preaching of the cross was in fact wisdom of a different kind—God's wisdom that brought about their rightstanding with God, their sanctification and their redemption (1:30). So he feels impelled to explain *how* it is that what appears so foolish to merely human eyes is in fact God's hidden wisdom, which is what 2:6-16 is all about. The answer lies with their common reception of the Holy Spirit. And note the irony here. They considered themselves people of the Spirit, the source of their present "wisdom." But Paul argues that what the Spirit really does is to reveal the message of Christ crucified as God's true wisdom. Thus Paul's contrast is not between spiritual and unspiritual Christians, but between those who have the Spirit and those in the world who do not. His point, as the transitional paragraph 3:1-4 makes plain, is that these very Corinthians who pride themselves in their spirituality, because of their experience of the Spirit, are acting precisely like those who do not have the Spirit, both by their behavior (i.e., their quarrels) and their failure to see that real wisdom lies in the message of the cross. Fine spirituality yours, is his point: you act like mere humans, who behave exactly like you because they do *not* have the Spirit—and you *do!*

With that point now in hand, Paul turns in 3:5-9 to correct their dreadful view of church leadership. Using the analogy of farming, Paul insists that their slogans quite miss the point. Their leaders are not lords to whom they may belong; to the contrary, they are merely servants of the farm, each with a differing task. Everything is God's—the farm, the growth of the plants and those who maintain it. In verse 9 he concludes, "We—that is, Apollos and myself—are workers together who both belong to God; and you, the church in Corinth, are *God's* field, not ours. So you simply cannot say, 'I belong to Apollos.' "

That brings us to our two paragraphs. At the end of verse 9 he switches metaphors: "You [meaning the church in Corinth] are also God's building." This is the metaphor that he will now use to make two more related, but quite distinct, points. In verses 10-15 he issues what has to be the strongest warning in the New Testament to those who are responsible for building the church. In this context it can only refer to those who are currently leading the church into its new folly of fascination with wisdom and rejection of the message of Christ crucified.

Paul makes two points. First he reminds them that the foundation for the church, which he himself laid, is the message of Christ and him crucified. To be legitimate, the superstructure must be built of materials that are compatible with the foundation. Second, the point of the paragraph is made in the warning in verse 10, "Therefore, let each one take care how he or she builds." Referring to the materials used to build Solomon's temple (1-2 Chron), he drives the point home that one can build with materials that are enduring or perishable, and that the test of fire will demonstrate which they were. His obvious concern is that those responsible for the continuing growth of the church in Corinth build with the imperishable material of the gospel. To build with wisdom, humanly conceived, is to build with wood, hay and straw. And come the day of test it will not endure, even though the workers themselves will be saved, but only as firebrands plucked from the burning.

Finally in verses 16-17, with a slight tilt in the argument, he pursues them all as to the nature of the building that they in fact are. Already hinted at in the building materials enumerated in verse 12, the explicit word of verse 16 is that they are God's temple in Corinth. Indeed, our use of the pronoun *you* for both the singular and plural has caused many a person to individualize this truly important community text. An expanded translation makes Paul's point plain: "Do you not know what kind of a building you are? That you, the church in Corinth, are God's temple (or sanctuary) in Corinth? And that such you are by the presence of the Holy Spirit in your midst? "Since that is so," he goes on, "if anyone destroys (dismantles) God's temple in Corinth, namely the church of the living God, God will destroy that person because God's temple the church is sacred to him, and that temple you the church in

Corinth are." Of course it is they who are in the process of dismantling God's temple by their wisdom and strife over their leaders.

This exercise demonstrates why literary context is so important. The local church is Paul's *only* concern in this text, not the individual Christian, either his or her life or body. He transfers this imagery to their bodies in the context of sexual immorality in 6:19-20. But the literary context, not to mention the meaning of the various words themselves, is decisive here. Here indeed is one of the most important texts in the New Testament as to the nature of the local church, and it is easily the most significant text as to its importance in the eyes of God. Along with the imagery of the body drawn elsewhere (10:16-17; 11:29; 12:12-26), this text serves as the first of the two crucial images of the church in this letter. What we can learn from such imagery is of eternal import.

Surely we need to hear this word in our own day—a day in which in the name of contextualizing, or cultural adaptation, the heart of the gospel itself is being given up for merely human wisdom, in which pagan values such as greed and materialism are being sprinkled with holy water and called Christian, or in which to get a hearing we insist on respectability, we insist on going first class. But our Savior suffered the ultimate indignity of a crucifixion. His apostle considered true discipleship as that which put him at the end of the triumphal procession of those who are destined to die in the arena (4:8-10). God's wisdom is still, and only, to be found in the scandal of the cross, where God in mercy endured the humiliation of human hostility. In that same mercy he used their very act of outrage against himself as his means of offering eternal pardon and forgiveness. That message, the apostle would insist, alone can lead to life. Any modifications to this are human wisdom and foolish in God's eyes.

The point still needs to be made that those responsible for building the church must make sure the "stuff" of the construction is compatible with its foundation. Build with the fluff of personality, charisma, contests, entertainment, and the local church will be ill-prepared to stand any genuine test of its faith. But build with the kind of discipleship Paul argues for in 4:7-13, and the gates of hell cannot prevail against it. Each of us must take care how we build, because the church is the apple of God's eye.

Finally there is the imagery of verses 16-17. The local church is God's temple, the place of his dwelling, his alternative to the pagan surroundings in which it is placed. Out there, there is greed, sexual immorality with its concomitant diseases, abuse of humans in the name of social class, you name it. Out there also, there is religion—plenty of it (twenty-six pagan temples and shrines in Corinth alone). "And such were some of you," Paul says in 6:9-11, "but no longer. You have been washed and justified and sanctified. Now you make up God's temple, the place of his presence in Corinth." In here, there must be the presence of the Spirit, in which his gifts build up the body and his fruit sbring healing to the hurting, forgiveness to the guilty, love to the alienated, joy to the sorrowing, peace to the troubled. If anyone destroys that by merely human wisdom or division, God will destroy such a person.

Questions of content. These are the *what* questions. We will illustrate them through 1 Corinthians 11:17-34, which refers to the abuse of the Lord's table in Corinth. We will focus on some *what* questions in verse 29; but we cannot look at those questions without at the same time making sure that we have the contextual matters also well in hand.

The answers to these questions usually require knowledge of the original languages. But one can get at the issues without knowledge of the languages by reading the text in several well-chosen translations, noting carefully where they differ significantly, that is, in a way that actually affects the meaning of the text. Because serious matters of understanding are involved, one will also need to consult some outside help.

The first context question is *textual,* having to do with what Paul in fact originally wrote. Look at verse 29 in the KJV: "For he that eateth and drinketh unworthily, eateth and drinketh damnation to himself, not discerning the Lord's body." Here is a text that has brought the fear of God, not to mention endless introspection and untold guilt, upon many a poor believer who feels quite unworthy to sit at the Lord's table. Notice how the two translations used by most evangelicals, the NIV and NASB, translate the first part of the text: NIV, "For anyone who eats and drinks without recognizing the body of the Lord"; NASB, "For he who eats and drinks . . . if he does not judge the body rightly." What is noticeably missing from both these translations and all other modern translations is the word *unworthily.* The reason for this is simple: it is not a part of Paul's sentence. It was added, first in the Latin tradition and then by most of the later medieval Greek manuscripts, under the influence of verse 27. And even there, it should be noted, the word does not mean "unworthy" in a moral sense, as if those guilty of sin are likewise guilty of the death of Christ if they eat at his table with such sin in their lives. This adverb in the Greek language means to participate at the Christian meal in a manner unworthy of the death of Christ that is here celebrated. Hence our text has not to do with eating and drinking "unworthily" but with eating and drinking in such a way as not to be recognizing (discerning) the body.

There is also a significant difference between the NIV and NASB. The NIV (as also KJV) says "not recognizing the body *of the Lord,*" whereas the NASB reads simply, "He does not judge the body rightly," without the additional words "of the Lord." This is a textual issue about which contemporary scholars are somewhat divided. These words, it should be noted, are supported by the same later and less trustworthy manuscript evidence that one finds supporting "unworthily." It also is a patently secondary addition to the text and *is not found in any of the modern editions of the Greek text.* The words were also borrowed from verse 27. "Bengel's rule" must prevail in this case: "That reading is to be preferred as the original that best explains the existence of all the others." In this case it is nearly impossible historically to account for the omission of the words "of the Lord" from the text had they been there originally. They clearly reflect how the early church understood the word *body* in this sentence, as referring to the Lord's crucified body represented in the bread at the table. It is hard to imagine how those words would have been eliminated in the early church had they been there originally. The question of text therefore is settled in favor of a Greek text that reads: "Whoever eats or drinks, not discerning the body, eats and drinks judgment on himself."

That leads us to the question of the meaning of words, and here we face the central issue as to the meaning of the text in its context. Two words demand our attention. To what is Paul referring by "body"? Is this a reference to the church, the body of Christ, or to Christ himself as he is somehow made present for us at the table in the bread? Related to that issue is the proper sense of the verb *diakrinō,* which ordinarily means to "discern, recognize or judge rightly."

Let us begin with the word *body.* It is easy to understand why the church has long believed that this refers to the Lord's crucified body, as it is made present for us in some way at the table through the symbol of the bread (and here there has been great debate in the church). After all, that has been a clear emphasis in the preceding verses. (In the words of institution in verse 24 the bread is specifically singled out as "this is my body," meaning "this represents my body." His body given over to death seems to be the only valid sense of that text. In verse 27 Paul says that whoever eats and drinks in an unworthy manner is liable for the body and blood of the Lord, referring to their assuming the same measure of guilt as those who originally crucified Christ.)

But there are a couple of reasons to give one pause at this point. First, in light of the immediate context, the usage in verse 29 is striking in two ways. First, it is the only absolute use of the word *body* without a qualifier in the entire passage. In every other case it is "my" body, or the body and blood "of the Lord." Second, it is also the only instance in the passage where there is no corresponding mention of the cup or the blood. Only here does Paul say simply "not discerning the body," with no qualifier and no cup/blood parallel.

Second, this usage now makes sense of an otherwise unusual short digression in 10:17. In the context of their being forbidden to join pagan friends at temple meals because of the covenantal aspect of their own Christian meal, Paul momentarily digresses and singles out the bread (alone) for interpretation, emphatically declaring that their partaking together of the one loaf was evidence that they themselves were therefore "one body." Note that this is the only occurrence in the New Testament of cup and bread in that order. Clearly Paul intends to say something about the meaning of the bread: "The bread which we break, is it not the fellowship of the body of Christ?" Paul asks. "For," he now adds by way of explanation, "since there is one loaf, we who are many are the one body because we all partake of the one loaf." Since that moment of interpretation played almost no role in the argument of 10:14-22, it is certainly arguable that it was intended by Paul to anticipate both this argument and that of chapter 12. Why therefore the absolute use of *body* in our sentence (11:29) should mean something *different* from what Paul himself says it means when *he* interprets our meal is what needs to be explained if he intended something different here.

This question obviously cannot be resolved simply by word analysis. This content question gets deeply interwoven with the issue of historical and literary context, to which we must now turn. The question is, Is this meaning for the word *body* and thus for the whole sentence supported by the context? The answer is yes, absolutely. Contrary to the practice of Communion in most Protestant churches, which begin the liturgy of the service by reading from verse 23 in our text, the real issue for Paul begins at verse 17, where he roundly gives it to them for what he says in both verses 17 and 22 is something for which he cannot praise them. They stand quite condemned because, as he says, even though it is the Lord's table that they should be eating, in fact it turns out not to be so at all. What happens when they gather for the meal, he says, is that they are divided (v. 18). But the context makes clear that this is not division along the lines of 1:12, over their leaders in the name of wisdom. Rather, the division is along sociological lines. He argues in verse 21 that their gathering represents an *idion deipnon* (a very private meal) rather than a *kyriakon deipnon* (a meal in honor of the Lord).

At this point we need to note some matters that pertain to the fourth content question, the historical-cultural background to the ideas expressed in verse 21. But before considering that, we need to examine how Paul himself views their private meals. It is with pure indignation. Look at the cascade of rhetoric in verses 21-22. It begins with the indictment, "One is hungry, while another gets drunk." To many moderns getting drunk is both unthinkable and intolerable, not to mention doing so at the Lord's Supper. But Paul is not so concerned about drunkenness per se. What he has done is to take words from both parts of a meal, eating and drinking, and express them in their extremes. The one extreme is for some to receive nothing to eat, thus to be "hungry"; the other extreme is to be gorged on both food and wine, thus to "be drunk." As the following sentence makes clear, Paul's concern is not with the drunkenness of the one but with the hunger of the other—especially in a context where fellow believers have more than enough to eat and drink.

Thus Paul (in our v. 22) bursts out with a series of rhetorical questions intended to reduce the "sated" to a level of shame similar to that to which they have reduced the poor. The first question responds directly to verse 21 and is full of irony: "For surely it cannot be, can it, that you do not have houses to eat and drink in?" That is, if you do not really have houses in which to eat your own private meals, then you are excused for doing so in the assembly of God's people. But if you are eating such meals deliberately in the presence (or absence) of others at the Lord's table, then a second question must obtain (and here is the key to everything): "Or do you despise the church of God by humiliating those who have nothing?" By this question Paul is getting at what for him is the real nature of their behavior, and so with a third (and fourth) question he brings the argument full circle: "What shall I say to you? Shall I praise you for this?" To which the answer is, Certainly not!

What lies behind all of this? How are we to understand the Corinthian abuse of the Lord's table? Here we need to spend some time with literature and evidence outside the New Testament. Two things seem certain from Paul's account: (1) the Corinthians celebrated the Lord's Supper as part of a regular meal of some kind, and (2) they were celebrating their own meal in such a way that the significance of the Lord's meal was being lost altogether, especially in the way that the "haves" were humiliating the "have-nots."

We know that the early churches met in houses, and that very often the houses were of the Roman style, with the rooms themselves forming something of a square around an open courtyard known as the atrium. One of the rooms, known as the triclinium (reclining at three sides of a table), was the dining room. We also know from the archaeology of Corinth that there were no houses—at least none has been discovered—in which more than twelve people could comfortably have reclined in the triclinium. If the triclinium was being used for these meals Paul is referring to, then only a select group could have been admitted, the rest being out in the atrium.

We also know that the Greek translated "one's own private meal" (v. 21) is technical language for the private meals of the well-to-do. The host tended to grade his guests, so that those of his own social class ate next to him and shared his privileged portions. The others tended to be graded into two groups: his lesser friends and his slaves or freedmen. For each of these groups there were different portions and apparently different starting times. This particular practice was so well known in the Greco-Roman world that it is spoken to at least seven times by ancient writers. The satirist Juvenal devotes one whole satire to this practice, which he disdains. His is obviously a view "from below." So too is the following epigram from Martial, who excoriates his host for treating him so:

Since I am asked to dinner . . . why is not the same dinner served to me as to you? You take oysters fattened in the Lucrine Lake, I suck a mussel through a hole in the shell; you get mushrooms, I take hog funguses; you tackle turbot, but I brill. Golden with fat, a turtledove gorges you with its bloated rump; there is set before me a magpie that has died in its cage. Why do I dine without you although, Ponticus, I am dining with you? The dole has gone; let us have the benefit of that; let us eat the same fare. (*Epigram* 3.60)

Here is the view "from above," where the elder Pliny is one of the privileged guests and is disgusted by it:

It would take too long to go into the details . . . of how I happened to be dining with a man—though no particular friend of his—whose elegant economy, as he called it, seemed to me a sort of stingy extravagance. The best dishes were set in front of himself and a select few, and cheap scraps of food before the rest of the company. He had even put the wine into tiny little flasks, divided into three categories, not with the idea of giving his guests opportunity of choosing, but to make it impossible for them to refuse what they were given. One lot was intended for himself and for us, another for his lesser friends (all his friends are graded) and his and our freedmen. (*Epistle* 2.6)

Although we cannot be certain, both Paul's language that "each one is going ahead with his own private meal" and the accusation that the "haves" are thus humiliating the "have-nots" and thereby despising the church of God suggest that something like this lies behind the abuse at the Lord's table in Corinth. We can envision a gathering at the home of Gaius, for example, in which he and his own social class are going ahead with their own private meal in the triclinium, while the majority, who would have been slaves or poor freedmen (compare 1:26), were basically excluded from the meal of the others and were thus excluded from the table of the Lord itself.

For Paul this is a double abuse. It destroys the meaning of the meal, where God's people together proclaim Christ's death until he comes. Part of that proclamation is found in the bread, whereby we declare that since all eat of the one loaf, we are all members together of the one body of Christ (10:17). By their meals they were negating the very purpose of Christ's death—to create a new people for his name, in which the old distinctions based on human fallenness no longer obtain.

Concluding our look at the historical and literary context, we may now return to verse 29 and observe how our prior lexical investigation is thus supported by the context. By their abuse of the poor at the table, the Corinthians are completely missing the meaning of Christ's body given over to death; by not properly recognizing the body—the church itself—in the eating of the bread, they are eating and drinking judgment against themselves.

If Paul is announcing judgment on them for their abuse of the body, why does he use the verb "recognizing/discerning," and what does it mean? The answer to this seems to lie in the wordplays on the theme of "judgment" that dominate the entire paragraph (vv. 27-32). No other form of this verb would be appropriate for expressing the need properly to take cognizance of the whole church that is seated as one body at this meal. The meaning here probably comes close to the English word *discern,* meaning to distinguish as distinct and different. The Lord's Supper is not just any meal. It is *the* meal, in which at a common table with one loaf and a common cup they proclaimed that through the death of Christ, represented in the elements, they were one body, the body of Christ. Therefore, they are not just any group of sociologically diverse people who could keep those differences intact at this table. Here they must "discern/recognize as distinct" the one body of Christ, of which they all are parts and in which they all are gifts to one another. To fail to discern the body in this way, by abusing those of lesser social status, is to incur God's judgment.

That is almost certainly what 11:29 meant in its historical context. The greater question for us is, What does it mean? How are we to appropriate it as God's word for us? Perhaps we Protestants could do better to maximize the point of this text. Our problem, it would seem, is precisely the opposite of that in Corinth. They were celebrating a meal in a way that lost the significance of the food. We, on the other hand, have kept the meaning of the food but have abandoned the fact that this food should be understood in the context of a meal. What makes a good meal, of course, is good food—and there is no better food for us than what is represented here at the Lord's table—and good fellowship. For Paul the bread expressed the fellowship of the body of Christ, where God's people affirmed their covenantal bonding to one another in Christ. Here there are no rich or poor, no Greek or Jew, no male or female. Here there can be no toleration of people being at odds with one another. "Because there is one loaf, we who are many are the one body of Christ." Thus at this table we must find ways to affirm that we are truly bonded to one another in Christ—and that we truly need one another, with all our faults and diversity.

At the same time, of course, with the cup we are reminded of the fellowship in the blood of Christ, the blood of the new covenant which was shed for us sinners. Here we again affirm and accept by faith that undeserving as we are, we are accepted in the Beloved. Our sins have been washed away; our guilt has been forgiven; our alienation from God and from each other has been overcome. Here we celebrate our common life in Christ that has been made available through Christ's death and resurrection and made present at this table through the work of the Holy Spirit. This is what the Lord's table must minimally mean; and what we all should learn from this text is the utter importance of recognizing and affirming the body as we eat together.

Thus our reasons for insisting that history is the first context for interpretation. Exegesis is a must, both because we will do it whether we like it or not (so we might as well learn to do it well) and because the nature of Scripture, God's eternal Word given in human words in history, demands it. With this series of illustrations from 1 Corinthians, I have tried to show the various steps in the exegetical process, while being deeply concerned at the same time to hear the word of God in 1 Corinthians and thereby to illustrate that good exegesis must always precede application.

I hope also to have illustrated that you do not need to be an expert to do exegesis well. The truly essential questions—those of context—are the open province of all. Even when you *do* need to go to an outside source for help with some of the content questions, you must always return to the text and make your own judgments in terms of context. Rather than taking Scripture out of the hands of the common person, as has been suggested, I intend quite the opposite. Since the Bible is for all, let all read it for life and growth. But let us do so intelligently, not willy-nilly or with a kind of laziness that gives credit to the Holy Spirit for every imaginable wrong interpretation of the text, simply because we were too lazy to do the hard work of study.

In any case, the greater difficulty all of us face with most texts is not with their meaning. That we can usually discern altogether too well. Our difficulty is with obedience; and here in particular we desperately need the help of the Holy Spirit.

2

Canon as Context for Interpretation

Elmer Dyck

T HE CHRISTIAN INTERPRETER has a canon with two testaments in it. The first is chronologically prior to the second, and despite the great many ways in which it is different from the second, both are descriptive of God's ways with his created world and, more particularly, with his people. Both testaments are, we believe, God's Word, his special revelation to the world. That is a theological given, assumed by the Christian church for nearly two millennia and articulated in many of its creeds.

The fact that the Bible exists in two parts rather than one is instructive. Traditionally both have been considered *equally* God's Word. Continuity as a very minimum was assumed from the start, even before there was a New Testament. The many quotations and allusions made by the New Testament writers testify, beyond question, to the fact that they saw themselves both defined and defended by the Old Testament Scriptures.[1] Its value was abiding. This they had learned from Jesus himself. The Scriptures (the Old Testament), he argued, not only taught about his coming, his person and his mission, but were, moreover, to define the believer's life "until heaven and earth disappear" (Mt 5:17-20).

While Jesus defended the continuing validity of the Old Testament, it is important to note that his teaching had raised doubts about that very thing. His "do not think that I have come to abolish the Law or the Prophets" was a direct response to those who had perceived in him an intention to do exactly that. Jesus' point was not so much that he stood somehow differentiated from the Old Testament (he was its fulfillment, after all) but that the Old Testament was being misunderstood. Immediately after his defense of the enduring value of the Law and the Prophets, he entered into a discussion of discontinuity, not with the Old Testament itself, but with traditions about its meaning. In addressing the issues of murder, adultery, divorce, oaths, retaliation and enemies (Mt 5:21-48), it was these traditions, couched though they were in biblical language, from which he distanced himself.

The Old Testament was the primary Scripture of the earliest Christian community. Its identity as God's Word was not doubted. Nevertheless, it was also understood that Jesus superseded the Old Testament, that Jesus' teachings about it stood somehow above it. He himself was its fulfillment. As is clear in the book of Hebrews, the Old Testament takes on the character of precursor, type, analogy, even shadow, of the *better* things revealed in Christ. "In the past God spoke to our forefathers through the prophets, . . . *but in these last days he has spoken to us in his Son.*" The difference is not only temporal; it is qualitative.

But it is also theological. The new covenant in Hebrews, for instance, is not just the fulfillment of an expectation, as it seems to be in the Synoptics. It is a signal to the death of the old. This notion of obsolescence is nowhere as clear as it is in Hebrews 8:13: "By calling this covenant 'new,' he has made the first one obsolete; and what is obsolete and aging will soon disappear." The writer is not referring to the Scriptures as such, but to a covenantal relationship between God and his people. Nevertheless, the Scriptures that define a now defunct covenantal relationship cannot hold quite the same function for the new people of God that it did previously. Its value now is primarily analogical.

None of this is to be seen as incipient Marcionism, for the writer of Hebrews never comes even close to abandoning the Old Testament. It is still God's speech, and he continues to use it as such, especially in the service of his apologetic and homiletical interests. But it is, nevertheless, a differentiated Scripture.

And so the titles given to the two testaments, old and new,[2] do distinguish the two: temporally (in that one is chronologically prior), qualitatively (in that one is the shadow of the other) and theologically (in that one defines an obsolete relationship with God and the other a new covenantal relationship based upon the redemptive work of Christ). But the one does not disqualify the other. The two remain in one Bible. Continuity and discontinuity are therefore affirmed, both in the New Testament itself and in the titles by which the two are recognized.

This belief in the oneness of the Bible, yet the differentness of the two testaments, had immediate hermeneutical implications. Was the Old Testament to be read on its own terms, without thought being given to the fact that the New Testament shaped the earliest Christian mind to think of the Old as promise or type, and therefore incomplete without reference to either Jesus or to the New Testament, its fulfillment or antitype?

The question is as modern as it is ancient. It is familiar to us all; we have heard this position argued from pulpits, in Bible study groups or in popular books on interpretation. But with the development of new historical sensitivities and methodologies that follow from them, we have become somewhat uncomfortable with this definition of the relationship between the testaments.

The problem is most clearly seen in our reading of the Old Testament texts. We, from the most conservative to the most liberal, have come to believe that texts are interpreted correctly only when seen against their immediate historical context. That is a legacy of the Enlightenment that we all share. We have been trained in this, not only in our universities, but also in our Bible colleges and seminaries. While we have all shared this belief, we have differed greatly over the details in the reconstruction of those contexts. The differences in reconstruction are not inconsiderable, but we will all defend the task and often employ similar if not identical procedures to assist us in that reconstruction.

Applying historical methodologies to Scripture soon forced hermeneutical questions back on us. We learned to argue that all texts, whether Old Testament or New Testament, are historically particular, that the writer of the text had a particular audience in mind, and that he intended to communicate a message for its benefit. We learned to do this with some success. The comfort level with our conclusions seemed to vary, however, depending on which testament we were interpreting. New Testament historical exegesis could be rigorously maintained because it was able to yield results that were generally reassuring and affirming of our theological heritage.

But historical exegesis, when applied to Old Testament texts, was not (and is still not) so uniformly supported. Aside from the fact that our traditions regarding the authorship and dating of books were challenged on every side by "the critics," we began to feel uncomfortable with some of our own interpretive conclusions, even in those instances where we were able to reconstruct a historical context more in line with our traditional or theological sensibilities. This was true particularly in our interpretation of texts that are quoted, along with an interpretation of their meaning, in the New Testament. More often than not, we were finding that our historically particular interpretations were at odds with those rendered by New Testament writers. We had reached one conclusion, but the New Testament writer argued another. Our theological sensibilities about the oneness of Scripture were especially under attack at this point. Put directly, history was in conflict with canon.

There are more than a few familiar examples. It is not at all obvious, for instance, that Hosea's reference to Israel's escape from Egypt (an event that occurred more than five hundred years before Hosea's own time) was somehow "fulfilled" in Jesus' return from Egypt as an infant (Mt 2:15); that the child of Isaiah 7:14 (Immanuel), whom the text clearly tells us will be born before the fall of Syria (732 B.C.) and Israel (722 B.C.) is in fact none other than Jesus (Mt 1:23); or that God's promise to Abraham that his seed (to be as numerous as the grains of sand on the seashore or the stars of the sky, if only you could count them) was really speaking of "one person, meaning Christ" (Gal 3:16). I could go on, but that will be reserved for the latter half of this study.

What are we to think or do when our historically conditioned reading is not that of the New Testament? Are we necessarily wrong in our interpretation of either the Old Testament text or the New Testament in its use of the Old Testament? Perhaps, and we need to take another look in order to correct what is demonstrably wrong. Or is the New Testament writer to be considered wrong in his interpretation, suggesting by the question that error on his part is but a reflection of his humanness? The very question, though it must be asked, jars the evangelical mind. The answer that rescues us at this point normally comes in the form of another question: Is there possibly more than one meaning to the Old Testament text, the first of which, being temporal, is recoverable by historical method, the second being more transcendent and therefore remaining dormantly mysterious, being recoverable only by means of special divine insight, even revelation? This question forces yet another: Ought we develop an approach to interpretation that is unique to the Old Testament?

The canonical approach, at least as I wish to define it, assumes that a text must be interpreted both in relation to its own immediate historical world and to the final shape of the canon. It assumes, to begin, that the historical approach is as appropriate to the Old Testament as it is to the New Testament. God's word to the Old Testament community is as particular to specific circumstances as it is to the New Testament community. It is no more mysterious or equivocal in its delivery than it is in the New Testament. We have not the slightest indication in the Old Testament that the message delivered in it was by nature puzzling, ambiguous or awaiting the clarification of another testament to give it meaning. If the Old Testament text had meaning to both writer and audience, it is that meaning that we mean to capture in our investigation. The historical approach alone equips us to do that. In this regard the canonical approach is thoroughly historical in orientation.

An interpretation in the context of the whole canon cannot, however, stop when an original meaning has been discerned, for several reasons. First, many Old Testament texts appear two or more times, once in what we might call an original context and then in an interpretive, usually New Testament context. The text has meaning in each context. Whether the meaning is the same or different from one context to the next makes little difference as far as the interpretive task is concerned. Each appearance must be examined in its own right.

Second, the Christian interpreter is not interested only in what words meant to another audience but in what they continue to mean to the believing community, today's believers included. God's word to a particular people in a particular time and place remains God's word to others and to us, people in widely divergent times and places. As much as we want yesterday's word to have meaning today, we must at the same time admit that seeking it can be a tricky business unless there is a control mechanism; the text cannot mean whatever we might wish it to. That mechanism, I would suggest, is the Bible's own interpretive tradition. It shows how old texts continue to function for subsequent communities. Where better to search for a model than within the canon itself?

Third, the Old Testament is not the entire Christian Scripture. To that extent it is incomplete; it begs a look at the larger witness, the witness of the complete canon. We are, after all, concerned to have the full canonical witness of God to guide and instruct us.

A History

The need to interpret the Old Testament in light of the full canonical witness has long been recognized.[3] The roots of such concern are found in the New Testament itself, in the way that Jesus interpreted the Old Testament in light of his person and mission. The New Testament writers almost without exception interpret the Old Testament in these terms.[4] So it was perfectly natural for subsequent Christian communities to perpetuate an interpretive tradition begun by the master rabbi Jesus and his immediate followers.

The canonical interpretation in the early postapostolic period was, understandably, harmonistic. The interpreters sought to explain the present reality (the gospel of Jesus Christ, or later that gospel as articulated by New Testament writers) through appeal to the duly established authorities of the past (the Old Testament). Old and New were unified in that both bore witness to the activity of God, and that the witness itself was from God. So the witnesses, the Old and New Testaments, were necessarily of a piece, in harmony with one another.

What this meant in practice, at least for the most part, was that the Old Testament was interpreted in the light of the New. The Old was promise, the New was fulfillment. The Old was shadow, the New was reality. The value of the Old lay principally in its witness to the New. Of itself it had little to say, so it was not, for the most part, heard on its own terms. One wonders, in fact, whether it was even perceived to have terms of its own. Its one true term of reference was the New Testament which it anticipated.

This assumption allowed a number of interpretive schemes to thrive. Whatever the method, it seemed that the Old Testament was perceived to say more (or sometimes less) than it appeared to on the surface. The particular methods simply articulated various ways of unpacking the fuller meaning (the so-called *sensus plenior*) of the Old Testament text. Perhaps the most common and most enduring of the early approaches was the typological approach.[5] Historical accounts were understood as historical accounts, not images that depicted some other reality entirely. But their value nevertheless lay in something beyond the bare historical account—namely, in the way in which the Old Testament events foreshadowed the later and greater events in which Jesus brought salvation to the world. The *Epistle of Barnabas* and Justin Martyr's *Dialogue with Trypho* are excellent early (second-century) illustrations of such reading. This approach continues to enjoy great popularity to this day. It redeems the Old Testament from charges of irrelevance and presents a unified picture of the whole Bible.

Typology both assured Christians and enabled them to answer charges made by two competing groups—the Jews and the Gnostics. As Joseph Trigg has said:

> Jews condemned Christians for retaining the Old Testament as Scripture but not observing the ordinances of the law. Gnostics, who contended that the God of the Old Testament was not the same deity as the God and Father of Jesus Christ, condemned them for retaining the Old Testament at all. . . . If, in opposition to the Jews it was necessary to show . . . that the Old Testament pointed toward and was superseded by the New, it was also necessary, in opposition to the Gnostics, to show that the two testaments were still in harmony. Typology . . . was well adapted to both these functions.[6]

Two schools of Christian interpretation soon developed. The so-called Alexandrian school was deeply affected by Platonic thought. It is hardly surprising that allegory was the primary mode of interpretation in this tradition. The Old Testament text, by such accounting, may have had a temporal earthly significance connected with the past, but its real meaning lay at another more spiritual level, one that reflected some aspect of the gospel of Jesus. The mundane earthly level had no enduring value. Origen, though later condemned as a heretic, established the foundations of allegorical interpretation that would dominate the Western church for centuries.

Both allegory and its cousin typology assumed either that the Old Testament writer did not realize the true significance of what he wrote, the text being a mystery which could not be fully understood until Jesus and the New Testament writers arrived on the scene, or that he did understand and that his audience could have understood had they not been so hard of heart. These assumptions seem to be alive and well in popular thinking, though writers like

R. T. France have argued for a much more carefully nuanced approach.[7]

But not all early interpreters were persuaded of the correctness of such approaches. The so-called Antiochene school of interpretation shied away from allegory, embracing a more literal or grammatical and historical reading which was believed better to represent the intention of the authors. Still, this school was probably not as antagonistic to the Alexandrian school as was once argued. For all their interest in historical and grammatical categories, the foremost leaders in this school, most notably Diodore, Bishop of Tarsus, remained deeply interested in the contemplative or spiritual meanings of the text. This higher level of meaning was not, however, discerned through philosophical categories as was conventional in Alexandrian thought. It was, rather, a disposition of mind.

The first three centuries of Christian interpretation set the agenda for centuries of Bible reading. *Methodologically,* the fourth to the fifteenth centuries witnessed very little change. There were, of course, many important developments. There were new adversaries to fight, new arguments to win. As the church established itself theologically, new matters of harmony arose. In order to deter false or heretical teaching, the church developed what came to be known as the rule of faith: Not only must parts of Scripture harmonize with each other, they must also be read in harmony with the established doctrine of the church. Scripture was the property of the church, and only the "legally competent" were to be admitted to it. But these are not methodological issues. On this score the allegorical approach gained the upper hand. It seemed to serve the more ascetic, mystical or contemplative focus better than any other. Augustine's dictum "The New is in the Old concealed; the Old is in the New revealed" expressed both the nature of the interpretation of the Old Testament and its relation to the New Testament.

The Reformation brought many changes to the face of the church, not the least of which was the way in which one read the Bible.[8] Much of the reading of the earlier Christian community had been made to conform to a developing dogmatic scheme or tradition, the so-called rule of faith. While all the Reformers challenged this tradition, none did so as forcefully as Luther. Scripture, Luther argued, should be taken on its own terms rather than largely on terms of the inherited tradition. *Sola scriptura* was his hallmark.

Luther did more than limit the interpretive parameters to Scripture alone. He also discredited the long history of allegorical interpretation in favor of historical commentary. But Luther did not break with the christological interpretation common to both typology and allegory. All Scripture, the Old Testament included, points to Christ. On these grounds he would argue that "Scripture interprets Scripture," one part (normally the New Testament) serving to clarify another (normally the Old Testament). So we see in Luther an interest both in history and in a canonical or harmonistic reading. History and the canon were the contexts.

We may well debate whether the Reformers succeeded in doing both well. Certainly they did it better than had most of their predecessors. And they did it better than most of their successors as well, since the momentum of the Enlightenment was clearly in favor of interpreting individual texts against history and not nearly so much against other biblical texts. In fact, the rationalist mindset of the post-Reformation era completely reversed the traditional relationship between faith and reason. Reason, earlier, was seen to serve and give cogent expression to faith. It operated within the sphere of faith. Faith defined the role of reason. For eighteenth-century thinkers like Spinoza, faith could not condition reason. Reason defined faith.

The history of the so-called biblical theology movement illustrates the hermeneutical implications of the supremacy of reason for a canonical reading of the Old Testament in particular.[9] The unity of Scripture could no longer be assumed. Scripture, even where the language of revelation was retained, was seen as an essentially human product. As such, a text's intention was nothing more than an author's intention, an intention, it must be stressed, that was shaped by the specific historical circumstances to which the author spoke. The message of a certain text might be quite different from, incompatible or even contradictory with another. Using criteria of reason, many such alleged contradictions were identified. A canonical reading of any kind was no longer acceptable.

It seems that the legacy of post-Reformation rationalism is as much with us as the legacy of Luther. What we might see in the more traditionally critical method is the tendency to read texts in historical terms only. Theology may matter, but it is of another order than history. Theological truth does not depend on historical truth. But the more conservative tradition is itself hardly exempt from this kind of rationalistic historicism. So-called liberals and conservatives are really very much alike in this regard. Both are driven by questions of historicity, both give priority to authorial intention, both use historical methods deemed appropriate to the enterprise, both defend their claims on rational (even scientific) bases, and both (although conservatives are loath to admit it) for these reasons have difficulty relating the two testaments to one another. Of course the actual positions argued are different, sometimes wildly, but the questions asked and the methodologies used are much more alike than either camp cares to admit.

Old style canonical reading has suffered greatly as a result. History seems to have triumphed over canon. Some (mostly at the popular level) continue to defend an approach in which the Old Testament is believed to mean what the New Testament says it means, based on the assumption that the Old Testament has a fuller meaning or that it has several layers of meaning. Others deny validity to such an approach but nevertheless come up with a final interpretation that looks very much like they did not really deny it all.[10] Both camps fail to give history and canon their full due. To this day, the Christian community remains confused about what to do with the Old Testament.

It is to the credit of Brevard Childs and James Sanders in particular that we have begun to develop a disciplined approach to reading both historically and canonically. While their individual contributions differ, the two have succeeded in moving us beyond the either/or of past interpretation into a both/and situation. The approach that I will be taking in this chapter is a synthesis of what I consider the best features of their work.[11]

Those features are (1) that the text is to be studied in its final form, (2) that the historical context from which texts originally emerged is by itself not an adequate context for exegesis, (3) that the canon itself is the context for interpretation and (4) that a description of the process by which texts and books are given their shape, though tentative, is nevertheless valuable.

1. Studying the text in its final form. Canon critics generally agree that most, or at least many, Old Testament books are the product of a sometimes long and complex process of development. In that respect they resemble the now-traditional historical critic. Given the task of exegesis, namely the investigation of texts set against the contexts out of which they emerged, books that for millennia had integrity as books suddenly became fragments reorganized according to the strata which mark their development. Genesis was no longer a book in its own right but a collection of teachings coming from three major sources: J which emerged in tenth century Judah, E in ninth century Israel and P in the restored fifth century community. Most of our technical introductions to the Old Testament do not even name Genesis but J, E and P in its place.

Childs will no longer be drawn into this enterprise, not because the description is altogether wrong (he himself doubts the independent existence of E but otherwise accepts the critical judgment) but because the sources are not the locus of authority. The church has always confessed a text in the final form in which we have it, not in some earlier stage in the process of its formation. But his reasons are not merely confessional. His argument is also based on the nature of the traditioning process (Childs, by the way, was at one point described as America's foremost tradition critic). The very nature of tradition is to ascribe authority to that version of the material that is current. Let us suppose, for the sake of argument, that the documentary hypothesis is correct. We would surely assume that when J and E were combined, both would lose their independent integrity to the new JE. Similarly, JE would lose its independent status when merged with P. And so on until we got Genesis. Exegesis, therefore, explains the text as we have it, not some hypothetically reconstructed source that lies behind it.

2. The inadequacy of historical context alone. While some Old Testament texts are very specific about the historical circumstances to which they refer, they may nevertheless be vague in the extreme about the contexts out of which texts actually emerged. The book of Genesis refers to the patriarchs. Whatever position one may take regarding the historicity of these accounts, one must admit that the text shows not a trace of interest in the context of the narrator of the accounts. Yet our exegetical task, as normally defined, tells us to be primarily interested in the narrator's context, the very context with respect to which the text is mute.

The canon critic is led to ask whether the task we have set for ourselves is in all respects appropriate to the nature of the material. The historian, as an analyst of events and their contexts, should certainly ask the question and make the best proposal the evidence, however limited, will allow. The exegete, as an analyst of texts, should take such conclusions into account, but should do so tentatively given the highly speculative nature of the enterprise.

But mere lack of evidence is not the only reason to be cautious. The reason for the lack of evidence is another. We know very little about writing conventions in ancient Israel (that is part of the historical problem), but we can tell from the literature itself that the writers tended to hide their footprints in the sand. They did not tell us why they did so, but we are probably safe in suggesting that they considered the context of the story to be more significant than their own contexts. They invited the reader to enter the world of the story, not the world of the author, saying in effect that the narration, though emerging in a particular context, is nevertheless at home in any and every subsequent context. The message, though delivered in a time-specific context, is, if you like, timeless. We might even say that was the intention of the author. If so, are we not being more true to authorial intention by shifting the focus from his context to the context to which he refers?

3. Seeing the canon itself as the context for interpretation. Seeing the canon as the context for interpretation assumes that the parts are integral to the whole, that the canon is a unity. The Bible is more than an anthology of books; it is itself a book in which all the parts cohere. There are many contemporary challenges to such a statement, based largely on evidence of apparent discontinuities (some say contradictions) between certain parts.[12] Still, those who were responsible for the collection of the materials we have in our canon saw in all its parts a message that cohered.

In practice this point means that a canonical reader will interpret an individual text in the larger light of others: first of all in light of its immediate literary context, then in the larger context of the book in which it stands, but then in relation to the collection of books in which it stands, then in relation to the whole rest of the Old Testament and finally in relation to the New Testament as well. This is the approach which I will follow in my own examination that follows.

All this bears considerable resemblance to the Reformation principle which argues that Scripture interprets Scripture. It is our concern to determine how it does that. Our conventional definition of the exegetical task, if taken seriously, would demand that only antecedent texts bear on the interpretation of another: New Testament interpretation must take the Old Testament into account, but Old Testament interpretation cannot take the New Testament into account inasmuch as it was not part of the Old Testament writer's horizon.

Canon critics say that we must take subsequent texts into account as well, not because they necessarily clarify an author's original intention (they may not), but because both the Old Testament text and the other, even later texts which draw on it, point to a common reality. Exegesis, by this definition, aims not only to explain a single text, but to describe the larger reality to which it points. Such a task is overtly theological and synthetic in nature. So an examination of the call of Abraham (Gen 12) is theologically incomplete without a further examination of the later Old Testament and even New Testament allusions to it.

4. *Recognizing the value in even tentative description of the process by which texts and books are given their shape.* While I could not go as far as Sanders does when he claims that the process is as canonical as the product,[13] I do acknowledge that the process, assuming for the moment that there was one and that we are actually able to describe it, has paradigmatic value. The process is hermeneutical in that it indicates how ancient texts continued to function for later communities. Texts have an afterlife, and the nature of the shaping process seems to have been such that they are made easily accessible to later audiences.

These are but general statements and illustrations. The rest of this chapter is a much more detailed examination of the familiar Immanuel passage of Isaiah, both in its own context and in the larger context of the New Testament, particularly the Gospel of Matthew.

Isaiah 7:14 in Canonical Context

The immediate context: a child as sign (7:1—8:10). This verse is part of a larger literary unit beginning at 7:1. Its ending is not as obvious, though it probably comes at 8:10. Its purpose is to announce the birth of a child who will function as a sign to Ahaz, the beleaguered king of Judah.

Ahaz's counterparts in Israel and Syria were Pekah and Rezin. These two had formed an alliance to stand up to the larger and increasingly more aggressive nation to the east, Assyria. They had seemingly invited Ahaz to join the alliance. He refused, probably thinking that the Assyrian assault was inevitable and that no alliance of small states would be able to resist her. Better to face the Assyrians as a neutral party than a self-declared enemy. As a result, the two kings to the north invaded Judah (probably more than once; see both 2 Kings 16 and 2 Chron 28). To aggravate matters, Judah was also being attacked by the Philistines from the west and the Edomites from the southeast. Surrounded by enemies, Ahaz had no apparent recourse but to join the alliance or to call for help from the outside. He chose the latter and called on the Assyrians, the very nation on whose account the states of Israel and

Syria felt compelled to consider military alliance. Apparently Ahaz thought he had less to fear from Assyria than from his two more immediate neighbors. Through this invitation, he declared himself a vassal to the Assyrian state.[14]

In this traumatic context Isaiah received a message to deliver to Ahaz. He should not be afraid of his northern neighbors. They are nothing more than two sticks of wood at the far edge of a fire which has more or less burned itself out. They will not succeed in their attempt to displace Ahaz with their chosen sympathizer, the otherwise unknown son of Tabeel.

It is not clear from the text what Ahaz was being asked to do in response to the threat. Clearly he was being encouraged not to give in to the pressure and join the alliance. He had Isaiah's support to that extent. But was he supposed to just hold out until the problem went away (as Isaiah suggested was imminent)? And if so, was he being discouraged from forming any counter alliances, such as he apparently made with Assyria? John Oswalt has argued convincingly that the book of Isaiah consistently argues against alliances of any kind, that Yahweh is Judah's protector. He called her into being, and he will sustain her.[15] It is no doubt for this reason that Isaiah enjoins Ahaz to stand firm in his faith (7:9).

Ahaz was not encouraged by the message. This is consistent with the description of him in both Kings and Chronicles. He was not known to be moved by the word of Yahweh. But he was given a second message (7:10-25). This second meeting with Isaiah was intended to confirm the message given in the first; namely, that Ahaz was not to worry. He was encouraged to ask for a sign, some confirmation of the prophetic claim that the two enemies to the north were not to be feared.

Ahaz declined the offer. His refusal has the appearance of piety—"I will not put the LORD to the test." But something else prompted him to answer as he did. He would not ask for a sign because he had already decided on another course of action: he would ask for help from Assyria. There was a superficial wisdom to this. By declaring himself both servant and vassal to Tiglath-Pileser, the Assyrian monarch, Ahaz was assured protection. And he was rewarded: "The king of Assyria complied by attacking Damascus and capturing it. He deported its inhabitants to Kir and put Rezin to death" (2 Kings 16:9). This effectively ended the immediate threat to Ahaz.

But Isaiah saw a greater threat to Judah's survival than the one posed by Syria and Israel. Ahaz would be expected to acknowledge his indebtedness to

Assyria by embracing that nation's entire political and religious philosophy.[16] And that he did. Temple worship in Jerusalem was made to accommodate, at least to some degree, Assyrian specifications which Ahaz had learned in his meeting with Tiglath-Pileser (2 Kings 16:10-18). But that was not all. Isaiah recognized that Yahweh would hold Judah to account for such apostasy by using the Assyrian for a purpose quite different from that which Ahaz had intended. Tiglath-Pileser might end the threat from the immediate north, but he and his successors would themselves become a threat to Judah's survival. "In that day the Lord will use a razor hired from beyond the River [Euphrates]—the king of Assyria—to shave your head and the hair of your legs, and to take off your beards also" (Is 7:20). On account of Ahaz, Judah would yet be humiliated at the hands of her deliverer.

Isaiah took Ahaz's refusal to request a sign for what it was and denounced Ahaz for trying the patience of both men and God. In his anger he announced that a sign was forthcoming anyway: "The virgin will be with child and will give birth to a son, and will call him Immanuel" (Is 7:14).

At this point the interpretation of this passage becomes controversial. Who is the "virgin"? Is this woman really a virgin at all? Who is the child? In what respect is the child a sign? Of what is the child a sign? While the text raises still more questions, it is these that concern the reader most directly. The answer to these questions is accessible to almost any reader. As much as we need to know is in the text itself. The fact that we struggle over these questions is proof, not of the inherent difficulty of the text, but of the influencing power of later interpretive texts, most notably Matthew's citation of this text as proof of the virgin birth of Jesus (Mt 1:23).

A canonical approach is very interested in the function that texts serve in the life of the believing community. The history of interpretation is integral to the approach. I am not so much interested in a complete history of the interpretation of this text (nor do I consider it in any way essential to the approach) as I am in the canonical history, the way this text continues to function in the understanding of biblical writers. Still, we commit a serious methodological error if we jump immediately from an Old Testament text to its New Testament use in order to discern what the text means. We will come to Matthew's citation in due course, but not before we have heard Isaiah on his own terms.

Let me begin my examination of this text by offering a literal translation of our text: "The young woman is pregnant and about to give birth to a son, and she will call him Immanuel." This text is familiar enough that the difference between this translation and most modern translations (the Jerusalem Bible and the New Revised Standard Bible being among the few exceptions) is readily apparent.

The Hebrew word *'almâh,* translated here as "young woman," is definite. It is not "a" young woman, as though she were any potential woman (so KJV and NASB), but "the" woman. Articles, in Hebrew as well as in English, bring particularity to nouns,[17] giving reason to believe that Isaiah has a particular woman in mind, someone likely known to Ahaz as well.

The word *'almâh* is better translated as "young woman" than as "virgin." Such a young woman was probably presumed to be a virgin, though that is not always clear from the texts in which the word appears. This word occurs only seven times in the Old Testament, and while translations will frequently render the word as "virgin," they do not consistently do so. Nor is there any compelling reason why in even one case they must do so. A brief look at each of the seven occurrences should prove my point.

The woman (Rebekah) who came to draw water from the well in Genesis 24:43 is simply referred to as a "maiden" (NIV). We do know that this maiden was a virgin, not because *'almâh* is used in this verse, but from an earlier reference (24:16) that specifically call her a "virgin *[bᵉtûlâh];* no man had ever lain with her." The sentence in 24:43 merely refers to her youthfulness as someone eligible to become a wife. The NIV translates the word here as "maiden." The "girl" (so NIV) mentioned in Ex 2:8 (Miriam) is probably a virgin, although the point is that she is young, still living with her parents, hence unmarried. The musicians of Psalm 68:25 are accompanied by "maidens" (so NIV) who play the tambourine. There is nothing else in the text that describes them, nothing that helps to define the word. The Song of Songs uses the word twice (1:3 as "maidens" in NIV and 6:8, "virgins" in NIV). The latter is the only other instance (in addition to Is 7:14) where the NIV translates this word as "virgin." Here the "virgins" stand alongside queens and concubines. It is apparent from this text that they are neither queens nor concubines and so are quite likely unattached to a man. The following verse again identifies three categories of women: queens and concubines as before, but this time, instead of rendering the third as *'almâh,* the text reads *bānôth,* "daughters." This parallelism provides a clue to the meaning of *'almâh,* namely that the person is youthful, at least relative to the queens and concubines. This fits the other uses we have examined, suggesting that the overall idea implied by the word is that the woman is young, unmarried and, by implication, not yet a mother. She may well be a virgin, but that is seemingly not the point that is being made.

Any possibility that the word must mean "virgin" is nearly eliminated by the one remaining use, namely, the woman mentioned in Proverbs 30:18-19:

There are three things that are too amazing for me,
  four that I do not understand:
the way of an eagle in the sky,
  the way of a snake on a rock,
the way of a ship on the high seas,
  and the way of a man with a maiden.

The reason that *'almâh* is not here rendered "virgin" is obvious. This "way of a man with a maiden" can be nothing other than a euphemism for sexual intercourse. If this woman is not married, she is certainly no longer a virgin. An *'almâh* may not be a virgin at all. At least in Proverbs, she may be assumed to be married. For this reason some assume that *'almâh* refers to a woman who has not yet born a child.[18]

Had the prophet Isaiah wanted to state specifically that the woman was a virgin, he would surely have qualified the word *'almâh* with further descriptive language or perhaps have used the alternative *bᵉtûlâh,* with or without further descriptive language. The language used of Rebekah in Genesis 24:16, for instance, is unequivocal: "The girl was very beautiful, a virgin *[bᵉtûlâh];* no man had ever lain with her" (NIV).[19] The fact that Isaiah did not use a qualifier suggests that youthfulness was more germane to what he had to say than was virginity. More than that, he would not have said that she was pregnant if he had wanted to say that she was a virgin.

Now we turn to the translation of the word *hārâh.* Most versions render the word as a future verb, "shall conceive," although it is actually not a verb at all. It is a predicate adjective modifying the subject of the sentence, *'almâh.* Because this is a verbless clause, we appropriately supply the present tense of the verb "to be." Hence, "the young woman . . . is pregnant." We have neither grammatical nor contextual reason to translate the word any other way.

"Is about to give birth" translates a Qal participle. Hebrew participles do not have any tense value in themselves; the time is determined by the larger context. Often, as in the case of the English present participle, the time is imminent. This suits the context well. The woman is pregnant; her delivery is not far down the road. The rest of the verse contains no real translation difficulties.

The young woman is not named, although (as already indicated) the article before the word suggests that she is likely known to both Isaiah and Ahaz. There are several possible identifications, but only one has good contextual support: that she is a wife to the prophet himself.

Isaiah 7 does not identify either the mother or the child. It describes a situation that is to obtain during a certain period in the child's development. "He (the child Immanuel) will eat curds and honey when he knows enough to reject the wrong and choose the right" (7:15). This sentence is less than clear by itself, though it should be noted that the diet of curds and honey is mentioned again in 7:22, the paragraph which describes circumstances that the people of Judah would experience when overrun by the Assyrians. This is, apparently, wartime food.

More helpful for our purposes is verse 16: "Before the boy [Immanuel] knows enough to reject the wrong and choose the right, the land of the two kings you dread will be laid waste" (7:16). In this context this "land" can be none other than the allied states of Israel and Syria. Clearly the boy is still a boy when these two states fall. We know that Syria fell almost immediately. The parallel account in 2 Kings 16:9 reports that Tiglath-Pileser himself laid waste to Damascus (Syria). That was 732 B.C. Israel collapsed exactly a decade later in 722 B.C. (2 Kings 17). While the child is not identified beyond the descriptive "Immanuel," he is prescribed by eighth century B.C. parameters.

Isaiah 8:1-10 provides, I believe, the answer to the identity question. Isaiah was told to write the words *mahēr shālāl hāš baz* on a tablet in the presence of important witnesses. The inscription is of obvious importance, although we are not told whether Isaiah himself yet understood its purpose. He "went to the prophetess," almost certainly his wife, and she conceived and gave birth to a son. She was told to name him Maher-Shalal-Hash-Baz. The tablet on which these words had been inscribed, we now understand, was nothing other than a birth certificate. This is the only instance in the Old Testament where we have reference to a birth certificate. The fact that it was witnessed by people of official position suggests that the birth is of great importance. That notice of it falls hard on the heels of the sign narrative suggests that the identity of the one is the answer to the identity of the other. The woman of 7:14 is Isaiah's wife, and the boy is his child.

Further support for this conclusion comes from the structural similarity between the two episodes of chapters 7 and 8. The child of chapter 7 will not yet be old enough to choose right from wrong when "the land whose two kings you dread will be laid waste." We read of the child in chapter 8 (Maher-Shalal-Hash-Baz) that "before the boy knows how to say 'My father' or 'My mother,' the wealth of Damascus and the plunder of Samaria will be carried off by the king of Assyria." The fact that the two predictions are virtually identical suggests that the children of the two chapters must at the very least be contemporary. Their juxtaposition leads us to suggest that the children are not just contemporary; they are likely one and the same child.[20]

Of course there are difficulties. Isaiah already had a son, Shear-Jashub, who had accompanied Isaiah on his first meeting with Ahaz in 7:3. How then could his wife be called an *'almâh,* even by the definition we have defended? Perhaps the Immanuel child was born to another wife. And why would Isaiah, in his sign statement, say that the woman "is pregnant" when it appears that Isaiah's wife became pregnant after the sign promise was given? We might answer that the Hebrew verb rendered "went" in 8:3 *(qārab)* could just as easily be translated as the pluperfect "had gone," and the "then" (the Hebrew *waw*) either translated as "now," or as grammarians now commonly argue, not translated at all. The remaining problems are, in other words, answerable. They are certainly not of such consequence that they would obviate the conclusions regarding the identity of the woman and her child.

Finally, it may be argued that the children of the two chapters, having different names, cannot be one and the same. Against that we may note that (1) the child of chapter 9 is given four names—none of them is Immanuel, yet interpreters have historically had no difficulty in suggesting the idea that Immanuel is a fifth—and (2) the word *Immanuel* actually occurs twice in connection with the child of chapter 8 (8:8, 10). This seems to be an intentional linking device, supporting the suggestion that the children are in fact one and the same.

This section tells us nothing about the child save his parentage and name(s). We learn nothing of his qualities or even his significance. We are not told that he will become a king or that he will hold any other office or that he will do anything special at all. All that we are told in this text is that his birth functions as a sign. Nor does the text state that any special circumstances attended his birth. Ahaz was permitted to choose just about anything, no matter how miraculous, that he would want as a sign. Having rejected his options, he was given this apparently simple sign. The birth seems ordinary enough, its importance lying principally in that it marked the time to start counting the years until Ahaz was to be free of his menacing neighbors.

The expanded context: a child as king (Is 9:1-4). Here we have another birth announcement. It is shorter than the former one and quite different in character. But before we look at it, we need to examine the transitional material between the two announcements.

Isaiah 8:11-22 consists of a divine word directed to Isaiah (vv. 11-15) and two exhortations from Isaiah (vv. 16-17, 18-22). Isaiah is warned by Yahweh not to be like "this people," possibly all of Judah though more probably Ahaz and his court officials. They are not prepared to rest their trust in Yahweh, having already chosen to align themselves with the Assyrians instead. Yahweh is a sanctuary to those who trust in him. To those who do not he is a snare. Trusting in any other, even the powerful Assyrian, will lead to certain ruin. Isaiah, with his sons acting as signs and symbols, then affirms his own loyalty to Yahweh. He calls the people back to what is certain, namely to the law and the testimony. Failing to do that, the people face nothing short of distress, darkness and gloom.

Chapter 9 begins by announcing that the anticipated gloom is now a reality; in fact, it is already near to an end. In the meantime, Yahweh had "humbled the land of Zebulun and the land of Naphtali," the Galilee. That the prophet should refer to this northern region as opposed to Samaria, capital of the northern kingdom of Israel, or to the nation of Israel as a whole, suggests either that the prophet has a particularly soft spot for the region or that the region is experiencing a darkness not shared by the rest of the northern state. The latter seems more likely. This text refers almost certainly to the annexation of these territories by Tiglath-Pileser III, king of Assyria.[21] It is from this darkness that the territory is to be relieved.

The oracle in 9:2-9 speaks to this situation. These are the people who have been walking in darkness. But they are also the people who have now seen a great light. The light is not identified, except that once again the political situation is informed by the birth of a child.

Who or what is the light over which the people are rejoicing? The light can be none other than the child described in verse 6 with respect either to his birth or his coronation. In any case, the identity of the child is cast back on us once again. The personal name is not given. We know that he is expected to reign on David's throne (9:7), meaning that he must be a Judahite of Davidic descent. And we know from the context that he is to be the answer to the pressing Galilean problem. These considerations greatly limit the range of possibilities, to the point that one can hardly avoid the conclusion that the next king on the horizon, Hezekiah, must be the person intended.[22]

The biblical witness regarding the birth of Hezekiah is most confusing. Second Kings 18:1 states that he began to rule in the third year of Hoshea king of Israel (ca. 730 B.C.) and that he was twenty-five years old at the time. According to such a calculation, he would have been born around 755, some twenty-two years before the annexation of the Galilee. On the other hand, 2 Kings 18:13 states that Hezekiah was in the fourteenth year of his rule when Sennacherib invaded Judah, ostensibly the year 701, meaning that he would have begun to rule in 715. Thus he would have been born around 740, some seven years before Tiglath-Pileser's invasion.

It is not my intention here to attempt a final resolution to this vexing chronological difficulty. Having suggested that Hezekiah is the child Isaiah calls the light to the Galilee, I cannot ignore the question altogether. Several factors which support my conclusion need to be taken into account. First is the very real possibility that the two calculations can be reconciled to each other. It may well be that Hezekiah began to act as coregent with his father Ahaz in 730 and that he took over as sole ruler in 715.[23]

Second, it should be noted that the text of Isaiah is announcing a birth, not promising a birth sometime in the future. The child has already been born. A comparison of several translations, say the NASB with the NIV, will highlight the different ways in which this text has been interpreted. The Hebrew renders the main verbs of 9:2-7 in the perfect tense, the tense which normally describes completed action. This is the way the NIV translates them: "the people walking in darkness *have seen* a great light" (9:2a). The NASB, however, translates them as though incomplete, as future. The reason for this choice, commentators tell us, is that the events described are manifestly future from the prophet's point of view. The Hebrew tense, though perfect, is to be viewed as the so-called prophetic perfect. The perfect tense, it is argued, may be used to express unquestioned certainty about the future; the writer is so certain the event will occur that he speaks of it as though it had already happened.

That the perfect tense may be used in such a way is accepted by most Hebrew scholars.[24] But since there is neither a special form for such a tense nor a special syntactical relationship that signals the use of such a tense, one is hard pressed to state when the perfect actually functions this way. No guidance can be given other than the demands of context. Need one interpret the perfect as a future in order to make sense, or at least better sense, of the text?

I would suggest that we err on the side of caution, rendering the perfect as a future only if the context *demands* it. For the context merely to *allow* it is not enough. In this instance, while it may be contextually possible to read these verbs as futures, there is nothing that demands that we do so. In fact, the more customary past tense makes more than good sense. The events described are not all manifestly future. One is compelled to appeal to the future only if one has already rejected the notion that the child is Hezekiah, maintaining that the child must refer to none other than the future Messiah. This is a theological commitment, neither a grammatical or historical conclusion that the text itself urges upon us. Literally and contextually rendered, then, the text of 9:6 states that the child "has been (or is) born."

Third, the text is less interested in the birth of the child than in his function. While we cannot be sure, it is not unreasonable to suggest that the language becomes a king's coronation as well as it does his birth. The newly installed king of Psalm 2, for instance, proclaims the Lord's decree: "You are my son. Today I have become your Father." If the analogy is valid, and I am satisfied that it is, then the actual chronology becomes virtually irrelevant. The concern is not with the year of his birth but with his coronation. Whether the year of coronation was 730 or 715 makes little difference because both make a great deal of sense.

A fourth consideration lies in the stated assurance that a king ruling on David's throne will resolve the problem in the Galilee. Hezekiah (assuming that he began to rule in 730, even if only as coregent) ruled over Judah as the nation of Israel collapsed (722). He would have been the first Judahite king to be in a position to do something about the north. We know from 2 Chronicles 30 that he invited the defeated peoples of the north to celebrate the Passover with the people of Judah. His invitation promised the northerners that if they returned to the Lord, the nation would be restored. He sent the invitation by courier to all parts of the northern territory, but almost everyone snubbed it. Among those who did welcome it, however, were people from Zebulun (30:11), people also identified in the Isaiah text.

Finally, it is very difficult to envision how any king later than Hezekiah could be imagined as an answer to the eighth century Galilean problem. A reading that identifies any other king as the referent of this text forces greater difficulty on the text than we face with Hezekiah.

The only serious argument against such a conclusion would be the exalted nature of the descriptive names used in 9:6. Would it be appropriate to use these names—Wonderful Counselor, Mighty God, Everlasting Father, Prince of Peace—of an altogether human king? Are they not be more appropriate to a king of another order, a divine Messiah?

Perhaps. But let us not forget that each social group has its own conventions about what is appropriate and what is not. It is not fair for us to assume that our conventions must necessarily have been the conventions of the biblical writers. The accumulated evidence of the Old Testament suggests, in fact, that Israel's view of their king was much less modest than the views that we hold of our leaders, royal or otherwise. Psalm 2:7, for instance, declares a newly installed king, presumably David, to be God's son. Psalm 45:6 goes even further, declaring that the throne the king occupies is divine. Such appellations, as all readers of ancient Near Eastern literature will know, were fairly common in antiquity.

None of the four names was actually inappropriate to a king, especially to a king of the Davidic line in whom great hopes were placed. In the word pairs that make up the names, one (sometimes the first, sometimes the second) modifies the other. Here *wonderful* modifies *counselor,* a word used of a broad range of leaders. *Everlasting* modifies *father.* The word *everlasting* is used of kings on more than one occasion to mean nothing more than that his rule will endure. (Note the NIV translation of the same Hebrew word *'ad* in Prov 29:14. "If a king judges the poor with fairness, his throne will *always be secure").* *Peace* modifies *prince,* a term befitting even a lesser leader.

The one term that seems inappropriate to kings is *Mighty God* (*'ēl gibbôr* in Hebrew), but the lexical evidence tells us that it is actually not inappropriate at all. We have already seen that the word *God* (*'ᵉlōhîm*) is used to describe the king in Psalm 45:6. The same word (*'ᵉlōhîm,* though more often simply *ēl)* is frequently used as a superlative adjective. For instance, the Hebrew of Jonah 3:3 reads that Nineveh was "big unto God." Most translations take that to mean that "Nineveh was an exceedingly large city" (NRSV). In at least fourteen instances the KJV translates the word as "power," "might" or "mighty (one)," or simply "great."

The full compounded name *ēl gibbôr* occurs six times in the singular and once in the plural. Scholars have often observed that in the compound the term always refers to God. That is true (our text remaining in question) only if one limits the data to the singular uses. The one plural use as found in Ezekiel 32:21 refers not only to mighty leaders, but to the mighty leaders of the mighty nations, leaders consigned to the pit together with Egypt. If this term can refer to the condemned leaders of foreign powers, then there is surely no reason why it could not be used of a godly Hebrew king.

Thus we see that the two texts I have examined leave us with several expectations. The first is that a child will be born who will signal the end of the Syro-Ephraimite threat to Judah. That child is Isaiah's own son Maher-Shal-al-Hash-Baz. He is important only because he functions as a sign. The second expectation is that a child who has been recently born or enthroned will free the region of northern Galilee from Assyrian control. That child is Hezekiah, quite another child than the one first expected. My approach to exegesis has been historical, the point of the exercise being to determine the meaning of the words as they would have been understood when they were first delivered.

A historical exegesis could easily stop at this point: two texts or pericopes have been identified, each being explained against its specific historical reference points. *Good* historical exegesis does not stop here since the picture is only partially reconstructed. The audience(s) heard more of the text than we have examined, and their minds and the writer's intentions were informed by that larger picture.

But what they heard in terms of content (historically and grammatically considered) and what the material says by the way in which it has been organized literarily are not necessarily one and the same. They (Ahaz in particular) heard, presumably first in oral address, two short messages in two different settings (the second is not described though it is introduced as distinct from the first). We find them, however, so closely juxtaposed that the distinction in setting is blurred. Three successive chapters (7—9) contain infant narratives. The first two, I have argued, help to explain each other. The child of the one chapter is the child of the other. But what is the relationship between the third and the first two? I argued that the third refers to another child, this one of royal blood, one who would act rather than simply be a sign. What is the relationship between these stories? Does the fact that they have been placed side by side have any bearing on how one reads them?

The question is complicated by the fact that we know so little about literary conventions in ancient Israel generally, and further that we know so little about the particular process by which Isaiah's spoken word was recorded to be read. Is it possible that Isaiah (assuming that it was he who both spoke the word and recorded it) placed these oracles side by side for no other reason than that they were both dominated by language of birth? Or is it possible that there is a chronological relationship between the two, that one birth comes hard on the heels of another? Or, suggested here with some daring, is it possible that the juxtaposition represents a kind of reinterpretation in which the two stories combined communicate (perhaps by design) something different from what they say when read separately from each other?

I could, in principle, accept the possibility of any of these options. None challenges my historical, literary or theological sensibilities to the point that I would have to exclude it. However, not all are equally likely. I cannot believe, for instance, that the stories are simply thrown side by side on account of verbal similarities with no intention to relate the two to each other in more substantive ways. More than a catchword theory is needed to account for this relationship. Nor am I convinced, in this case, that the two are juxtaposed to somehow qualify each other or to effectively alter the meaning a text had historically. The two children, for instance, cannot by the mere fact of juxtaposition suddenly be imagined to be one and the same child. I am troubled by the suggestion that the intention of a prophetic oracle could so easily be suspended. For these reasons I believe that the second option seems to explain best the nature of the relationship.

A canonical interpretation cannot stop here, if for no other reason than the fact that texts are part of a larger context. Space prevents us from examining all the contexts. To be complete we would need to examine Isaiah 7—9 in the light of the rest of Isaiah, then in the light of the rest of the prophetic literature and the whole of the Old Testament and then finally in the light of the New Testament. For the purposes of this essay I will move directly to the New Testament, recognizing, of course, that the canonical task will not be completed.

The New Testament context. Isaiah 7:14 is cited in Matthew 1:23. Literally translated it reads, "Behold, the virgin will conceive and give birth to a son and they will call him Immanuel." The Greek word *parthenos* refers not just to a young woman of marriageable age but very specifically to a virgin. Had Matthew been satisfied merely to stress youthfulness, he would have likely used the less definite word *neanis* that means simply "young woman." Though Matthew does not cite the LXX verbatim, he does seem to follow it in the translation of this word. The other early Greek translations all depart from this reading by translating the Hebrew *'almâh* with the more general term *neanis.* It is also worthwhile noting that both the LXX and Matthew retain the definite article, meaning that the virgin is specific. The versions disagree on who does the naming. The Hebrew reads "she," meaning the young woman herself. Matthew has an indefinite "they," which is the active equivalent to the passive, "he will be called." The LXX, on the other hand, reads "you" (singular), with Ahaz being the antecedent. One might gather from this that the LXX translator understood that the child was to be the king's own son, presumably Hezekiah.

Matthew quotes this text to explain how the birth of Jesus came about. Mary, we are told, had become pregnant by the Holy Spirit. Joseph, assuming the worst, was set on a quiet divorce. An angel appeared to him, partly to defend Mary and partly to announce the nature of the child and his task: "She will give birth to a son, and you are to give him the name Jesus, because he will save his people from their sins. All this took place to fulfill what the Lord had said through the prophet" (Mt 1:21-22 NIV).

"All this" apparently refers to the concern over Mary's pregnancy; that is, to the identification of the child's father. The issue is not so much whether or not Mary was a virgin, but who is the father of the child. Satisfied that the Holy Spirit and not some other man was the father, Joseph dropped his divorce plans and "took Mary home as his wife." The point I want to make is that the purpose of the citation is not to prove a virgin birth (though that seems, by implication, to have been the case) but to prove divine parentage, that the child is the son of God.

The second Isaiah text is cited in Matthew 4:15-16: "Land of Zebulun and land of Naphtali, way of the Sea, alongside the Jordan, Galilee of the Gentiles: The people walking in darkness have seen a great light; a light has dawned on those living in land of the shadow of death." There are no difficulties in the translation. The rendering of Matthew accords very well with the Masoretic Text of Isaiah 9.

The point of this citation is to explain Jesus' move from Nazareth to Capernaum. The move was, in fact, a fulfillment of what was said by the prophet Isaiah. Jesus is the light to the Galileans, to those living in darkness.

We therefore conclude not only that Matthew sees the two children of Isaiah 7—9 as one and the same child but also the one child is none other than Jesus, neither Maher-Shalal-Hash-Baz nor Hezekiah.

The difference in understanding between Matthew and my historically conditioned interpretation is considerable. Or is it? Is Matthew really citing these texts as proofs, as fulfillments of Old Testament prophecies? A look at Matthew's wider use of the Old Testament is instructive.

Matthew is rather formulaic in his citation of Old Testament texts. Most of his quotations are signaled by the words "these things happened so that what was said by the prophet might be fulfilled" or something very close to that. Much of Jesus' life is described in these terms. So what does Matthew mean when he says that Jesus is the fulfillment of various Old Testament expectations? Does he mean that Isaiah made a prediction that someone would be called Immanuel and that now, finally, in Jesus, that one has appeared? That someone would come as a solution to the Galilean oppression and that someone, again in the person of Jesus, has now appeared?

That is what the word *fulfillment* normally means to us. Is that what it meant to Matthew as well?[25] Perhaps. But let us consider a few specific texts in Matthew that suggest otherwise. The first is Jesus' statement that he is the fulfillment of the Law. Now law is not a prediction at all, though it does indicate by its very nature that it expects something. People will either observe it or they will not. But the Law is not particular to any one person. Observance was expected of everyone in the covenant community.

So what did Jesus mean when he said he was the fulfillment of the Law? He certainly did not mean that he would bring it to its conclusion, as if to say that the Law would cease to be important. Not at all, since he also said that he did not come to abolish the Law. What he meant, then, was that he would observe it, that he would observe it well, in the spirit in which it was intended. So he is the faithful Lawkeeper, one who fulfills or satisfies its expectations. One cannot help but sense that Matthew records this teaching of Jesus for comparative purposes. Jesus keeps it as none other, in fact as all

Israel had failed to keep it.

Or take Matthew's curious use of Hosea 11:1. The visiting magi had asked Herod where the child born to be king was to be found. That question set Herod's mind to spinning since he was in no mood to entertain a usurper. So he undertook a vicious campaign to kill any and every possible contender—all children under two. Jesus, Matthew tells us, was taken to Egypt by his parents to escape the threat. He remained there until Herod died, and at the notice of an angel was taken back in safety. All this, Matthew assures us, happened to fulfill what was said by the prophet: "Out of Egypt have I called my son."

Our common view of fulfillment would have us believe that in Matthew's view, the prophet had predicted that God's son (and that could, of course, be none other than Jesus) would be taken to Egypt and later returned; that had now happened, as predicted, to Jesus. I find that this view stretches credulity more than a little. Not because the prophet could not utter predictions that would come true, but because the prophet clearly tells us who the son was, namely Israel, an Israel who was unfaithful from the day God tried to teach them to walk. Surely Matthew had read the context of the text he was quoting and knew all this.

So what did Matthew mean when he said that Jesus is the fulfillment of this text? It seems to me that he meant nothing more than to suggest that Jesus, like Israel, had come out of Egypt. Once again Matthew is being comparative or analogical in his use of the Old Testament, and once again Jesus is what all Israel was not. The true, or perhaps representative, Israel has come out of Egypt. In this latter Israel one can have more confidence than in the former.

This is what Matthew does quite consistently. Jesus is compared either to the nation or to individuals in whom high expectations were placed and, at least in many instances, proves to be what they were not. This, it seems to me, is what Matthew was doing with the Isaiah texts as well. Jesus is like Immanuel (or Maher-Shalal-Hash-Baz) in that he is a sign of God's presence to a people under threat, people who need to learn to rely on the God who is with them and not on some desperate scheme to win them peace and security. Similarly, Jesus is like Hezekiah in that he forecasts the possibility of release from bondage (albeit in quite another way) for the people of Galilee. He is the light.

Interpreters over the years have sought to explain Matthew's use of the Old

Testament in any number of ways. The more recent way uses the Qumran approach to reading the Old Testament, which we normally call *pesher* or *midrash pesher*. This approach is situated squarely in the current tradition of seeing texts (such as Matthew) in their historical and cultural environment. Matthew, so it is said, follows the pattern of the Qumran covenanters in lifting the Old Testament text out of its historical moorings and making it apply directly to his situation and no other. The Old Testament text is mystery (the Qumran word is *rāz*), but its interpretation (the Qumran word for this is *pesher*) has been revealed to the inspired interpreter Matthew. The interpretation applies to the present only, most particularly to Jesus. And because Matthew does not exegete the Old Testament text as we teach our students to, he is sometimes accused of twisting the Scriptures. He makes the Old Testament mean what it does not and cannot mean in its own context.

It should be obvious that I have no difficulties with a historical interpretation of texts. That is what I have insisted on doing with the two Old Testament texts I have examined. Nor are my theological sensitivities rankled when I am told that Matthew's interpretation of Old Testament texts is at odds with the original meaning of those texts. But I am not satisfied that this describes what is happening here. Nor, for that matter, am I satisfied with the more traditional approaches.

These other approaches are more self-consciously canonical inasmuch as they seek to interpret the Old and New Testament texts in light of each other. One approach (like the one above) suggests that the Old Testament text is essentially mysterious and that it awaits the explication of the New. Neither the original author nor his audience could grasp the message, at least not fully. A twist on this approach is the assumption that the audience really did understand the text but that their hardness of heart kept them from believing it. By this accounting Isaiah's texts (whether he and his initial audience knew it or not) referred always and only to Jesus. My own historical reading would be completely disqualified.

Some have granted that the Isaiah texts actually point to some contemporary fulfillment, but only in the first instance. The text, it is argued, has more than one fulfillment, and any of the first hearers would have judged the text to point to some ultimacy far beyond its first fulfillment. So the Immanuel text refers in the first instance to Maher-Shalal-Hash-Baz (or as some would argue, Hezekiah) but it also implies an ultimate fulfillment in the Messiah.

This approach emerged, I suspect, largely out of theological convenience, its concern being to rescue the Bible from conflict. It is first and foremost harmonistic in nature.

Modern hermeneutical theory often argues for multiple meanings. Language is polyvalent, the meaning of particular linguistic constructions variable. This is a theory that can accommodate a number of the approaches to Matthew's use of the Old Testament text that I have noted. I am prepared to grant some credibility to such a theory, at least in principle. But I will not allow it to be invoked as a matter of convenience. We could never achieve certainty about the meaning of any text if we assumed multiple meanings as a matter of course. Nor do we read this way with any degree of consistency. We tend towards it only when our historically conditioned reading of the Old Testament comes into (apparent) conflict with the interpretation rendered by a New Testament writer.

The approach to canonical interpretation that I have proposed rescues us from the weaknesses of the other approaches. It is thoroughly historical in its examination of the text in both its Old and New Testament contexts. It assumes that authors have intentions, that the intentions were understood by the first audience, and that these intentions are (for the most part) recoverable (even though in most cases extremely remote) through the application of appropriate historical tools.

Merely noting how Matthew uses the Isaiah texts is not being thoroughly canonical. Most of what I have done with both the Old Testament and New Testament texts in this study is distinguishable from a purely historical approach only in that I have even bothered to read the New Testament text when my goal has been to understand the Old Testament. But it is canonical to the extent that I have, in the interests of finding a paradigm for reading, dealt with the function of a text in the life of a later community of faith. Matthew does not seem to have done a careful exegesis of the Isaiah child narratives, at least not in the way in which we normally use the term. That was not his goal. His intention was, among other things, to show that Jesus is the true and superlative Israel, like the son but greater, like Maher-Shalal-Hash-Baz (Immanuel) but greater, like Hezekiah but greater again. Matthew's reading is analogical, demonstrating that Jesus has become what no other Israelite has, that he has satisfied the expectations and so deserves to be the ruler of Israel. He is that greater David whose right it is to rule.

The ultimate goal of the canonical approach is to consider the reality to which the texts point. The approach assumes that while the two testaments are indeed two and not one, that they are distinct and are to remain distinct, they nevertheless speak to one reality, namely God's gracious dealings with his creation. No examination of texts is complete without such a theological reflection.

These texts assure us, more than anything else, that God is with his people: Immanuel. His being with us is not always a comfort. Ahaz was to be encouraged by the sign. It was Isaiah's intent to assure the king that God would protect him against his northern neighbors, if only he would trust in God. But the sign, given to the king who did not even want it, turned out to be something less than an assurance. It was delivered in anger (he had tried the patience of both the prophet and God) and now bore more than a hint of warning, an ominous note that God would in fact use the Assyrians, with whom Ahaz had made an alliance against Israel and Syria, but that he would use that nation to deliver a serious blow to Judah as well. It is interesting to note that the two other references to Immanuel in these chapters (Is 8:8, 10) are both in the context of judgment. God was with Ahaz, not to help but to judge. In this respect the words "God with us" are like the Old Testament "day of the LORD." This term had once suggested hope and comfort but had now been turned on its head (Amos 5:18-20).

The child narrative of Isaiah 9 tells us that God's presence is essentially hopeful and not judgmental. He will be with them in the person of a righteous king and deliver them from the tyranny of the enemy, indeed the very same Assyrian enemy that he used to judge in the first place. Even judgment has a redemptive character to it. Matthew draws on both images. Jesus, the New Testament Immanuel, will save people from their sins. He is also the light to the Galilee, preaching repentance since the long awaited kingdom was near. Repentance was what Isaiah had wanted from Ahaz but what he did not get. That in mind, one wonders how the Galilee will respond to Jesus. Will he be to them a savior or a judge? Another Matthew text suggests the latter: "But I tell you that it will be more bearable for Sodom on the day of judgment than for you" (Mt 11:20-24).

It would be simplistic to suggest that a canonical approach is really nothing more than a new name for the older typological approach. It would be equally simplistic to deny that it does, in fact, draw heavily on this older approach, at least where judiciously practiced. Typology serves the goal of a canonical approach in that it provides the reader with a set of texts which together point to a common reality. And it should comfort us to know that this is how Matthew is using the child narratives of the book of Isaiah.

It should please both scholar and preacher to know that exegesis can be done with full seriousness, and that the end result can still be preached. Canonical exegesis aims to serve the church. It is no coincidence that the forgers of the approach, both Childs and Sanders, were both high-ranking scholars and ordained churchmen. Other churchmen, coming from a variety of denominational and theological persuasions, are finding it a welcome answer to the two very different but equally one-sided concentrations on either history or canon. This approach resorts to neither strained harmonization nor notions of fuller meaning to hear the Word of God in its full canonical context.

3

Theology & Bible Reading

J. I. Packer

I HAVE WRITTEN elsewhere[1] of a decision I came to at the ripe old age of eighteen. Having been a Christian for less than a year, I told my Oxford College chaplain, a devout high Anglican, that I did not want to study theology because it would not help my faith. Why did I utter such discourteous rubbish? I wince every time I think back to it. Well, rubbish in the mouth argues rubbish in the mind, and the rubbish in my mind at that time was a half-truth which, through being taken as the whole truth, was functioning as a falsehood. (Half-truths do that; be careful!) My thought was that since the Bible contains in itself the principles of its own interpretation (true), and since the Holy Spirit who inspired it enlightens humble hearts to see its meaning (true again), all the secrets of Scripture would yield themselves up to me if I simply prayed and read the text.

But this is a drastic oversimplification. *Some* of the Bible's secrets would certainly become clear to me that way. Many Bible readers, past and present, could testify to precious lessons learned through soaking themselves in the text and letting one passage throw light on another. But *all* of the lessons, or rather, all that I need to know of them? No! I need help from the church's ongoing theological life, and from theology itself, or at crucial points my understanding will fail. What I did not grasp when I was eighteen was that God intends us to learn what he teaches in the Bible, not through isolated independent study, but through sharing in the intellectual give-and-take of the church's fellowship. This means sermons, books, arguments, discussions. It means nurture for the mind as a basic element in the discipling process. It means, in other words, theology.

In those days I pictured the church's theological life in terms of clergy chasing black cats in a dark cellar ("why don't they just believe the Bible and stop asking these questions?"), and I thought of theology as a rickety and flawed human product, the fruit of intellectual worldliness and pride, a corpus of needless complications that could only block the path to spiritual understanding. These ideas were stupid (there are few stupidities that I have not embraced at some time or other), but my observation of congregations, parachurch groups, Bible colleges and seminaries convinces me that many Christians' minds are still in their grip. My bold prejudice against theology as an aid to Bible study, and my old belief that the best Bible study is done without it, seems (for instance) clearly to underlie the routines taught nowadays for "inductive" Bible study, just as a generation ago it underlay the ministry of those who called themselves Bible teachers as distinct from theologians. This is bad news.

In the following pages I shall try to blow this impoverishing prejudice out of the water by showing, on the one hand, how unstable, unchurchly and indeed un-Christian a thing is Bible study without theological ballast, and on the other hand how theology illuminates the height and the depth and breadth, doctrinal, ethical, devotional and apologetic, of Bible reading. A tall order? Well, let us see how we get on. I start with two basic questions.

What Is Theology?

The first question I shall address is, What is theology? *Theology* ("thought and speech about God") is a science, a branch of knowledge regarding matters of fact. The subject of theology is God the Creator, the living Lord, as he stands related to everything that is not himself—ourselves included and indeed highlighted because the Bible centers on God governing, judging and saving humankind. Like any science, theology as it exists today is a continuing cooperative enterprise with a history of development and a set of established techniques of investigation. What holds the enterprise together and gives it its continuing identity is the questions it aims to answer. Physics asks, How does the natural world system work? Biology asks, How do the various lifeforms work? And theology asks, How does God work?

Each science has its own appropriate method for answering its own question. Physics and biology go and look, making observations, setting up experiments and reading off the results, "putting nature to the question" as Francis Bacon expressed it, to find out what happens under different conditions and circumstances. Theology, however, listens and judges, letting the Bible speak in its own terms about the whole of life and then interact with what both the world and the church and the individual student have said and are saying, and also have done and are doing. Each science seeks truth; but whereas physics and biology pursue empirical truth about creation in order to harness it technologically, thus using it for human benefit, theology pursues revealed truth about the Creator in order to know him relationally in a life of worship and obedience, thus using truth for his glory and for the correcting and directing of our thoughts and ways in his service.

To come a little closer: theology is an organism of thought, a complex of disciplines (that is, procedures, each with its own rules and resources) that feed and are fed by each other. Because everything in theology has links with everything else, nothing in theology is sufficiently understood the first time you meet it: only when you have explored its links and seen what it presupposes and implies do you begin to grasp it adequately. Someone once said that Jane Austen's novels, subtle and beautifully wrought as they are, should first be read for the fourth time; in other words, only at the fourth reading can you properly appreciate them—and the same sort of thing has to be said about our study of theological truths.

Theology, with its network of internal linkages, has sometimes been described as a circle or (better) a rising spiral, the thought being that until you have toured the whole of which each item is a part, your understanding of that item is certainly deficient. But when you come back to it after making the tour, you understand it at least a little better than you did before. Making the tour, or going round the circle, means tapping all the disciplines that make up the organism of theology to see how their subject matter and working hypotheses bear on the particular perception that was your starting point.

The organism of theology used to be analyzed as a quadrilateral. First came biblical theology (exegesis of texts and synthesis of findings). Then followed systematic theology, including ethics. Church history including historical theology was discipline number three, and practical theology, covering spiritual life, pastoral care, preaching and worship, brought up the rear. But this classical analysis is too dense for comfort. It will be clearer if we distinguish within theology the following ten disciplines.

1. Exegesis. Exegesis is the foundational activity. Exegesis seeks to answer the question, What was this biblical text, passage or book written to convey? What was the human writer telling his envisaged readership about God and human beings under God, and so about himself and themselves? Only when exegesis has shown what a passage *meant* as communication on the human level can we hope to discern the universal truths about God and man that are embedded in it, apply those truths to our own situation, and so see what it *means* as a word from God to us. *Interpretation,* the process of showing the meaning of Scripture as God's word to present-day readers, begins with exegesis and is completed by application.

2. Biblical theology. Biblical theology is the discipline that synthesizes and organizes the findings of exegesis, both topically and historically. It seeks to answer such questions as: What is the total message of each biblical writer about this and that and God and godliness? What is the total message of the whole Bible about these matters? By what stages was this message revealed? How much of the total revelation is presupposed by each writer when he says the things he does? All questions of the interrelation of the teaching of one part of Scripture with the teaching of another part come under the scrutiny of biblical theology. It is a unifying, integrating discipline.

Two modern fashions among academics that muddy the waters for biblical theology should be mentioned here. One is the insistence that every church and theologian works not from the Bible as a whole, but from a "canon within the canon." On this it suffices, I think, to comment that insofar as they do this it is not a virtue but a weakness, which more attention to biblical theology should help them to overcome. The second is the habit of forcing one Bible writer's theology to contradict another's, and of representing different verbalizings of the same truth as if they were mutually exclusive. If one weighs the fact that all Scripture is ultimately the product of a single mind, if one remembers that it is possible to give the same thoughts different verbal clothing without them thereby ceasing to be the same, and if one then looks dispassionately at the evidence for supposedly incompatible theologies, one is likely to end up skeptical of this trend and wishing that those professional biblical theologians who currently hunt for internal disharmony with such diligence might soon tire of their unproductive game. The theological unity of the New Testament, indeed of the whole canonical Bible, is one of the most remarkable things about it, and one longs for the day when scholars will be celebrating it again.

3. Historical theology. Historical theology is at the heart of the discipline of *Christian history* (the formula "church history" is really too narrow for the story of God's people living by God's word in God's world). It explores how Christians in the past viewed this or that element in the biblical faith, and how they grasped, affirmed and defended that faith as a whole. What were their questions? Their answers? Their certainties? Their problems? What challenges were they up against, and what influences, both conscious and unrecognized, were they under as they did their thinking? Believers go into these matters, not just from friendly interest in those who were in Christ before them, but because wisdom tells them to learn from the achievements of the past. Modern students of physics or biology do not have to reinvent these sciences because they receive from the past, along with developed techniques of inquiry, a massive array of solidly researched conclusions from which in due course their own experimental work will begin. Their heritage kick-starts them. And so it is with theology. The two-thousand-year heritage of discussion and discovery within the church is called "tradition." It is not infallible and sometimes needs critical correction from the infallible Scriptures on which it is based. But for all that, it has permanent value as a well-explored preliminary attempt to expound and apply Scripture for the guidance of others. If we ignored it, spurning the help it could give, we should be total fools—sure of our self-sufficiency, yes, but fools all the same because self-sufficient we are not. Historical theology exists to save us from this kind of folly.

4. Systematic theology. Systematic theology gathers to itself the findings of exegesis, biblical theology and historical theology in a watershed discipline. It is what we have been coming up to in all that we have discussed this far, and all the disciplines still to be mentioned will draw down from it. Systematic theology thinks through the material that biblical and historical theology present in order to find a way of stating the whole faith today, topic by topic and in all its fullness, that will show its coherence and cogency in relation to current interests, assumptions, questions, doubts and challenges, both outside and inside the churches. Some have chosen to call the discipline dogmatic theology on the grounds that it deals with the defined faith (the dogmas) of the church, but "systematic" says more about its scope and style and is therefore preferable.

In idea, at least, systematic theology shapes both the confession of faith that individuals and churches make and the life of faith that they live before the unbelieving world and before the Lord. It formulates the faith in language that is biblically based and contemporary in thrust. When properly managed, it appears as a discipline of declaratory and applicatory biblical interpretation which merits the description "systematic" not because it imposes a speculative system (it does not) but because it thinks biblical themes together in the way that Scripture itself does and sets forth each as part of a God-centered, thought-out, self-consistent whole. Good systematic theology always commends itself as a testimony to the God of the gospel, the triune Creator-Redeemer, and as a transcript of this God's self-disclosure and of the revelation of his mind as set forth in the Bible.

It is true that speculative religious schemes, only loosely linked with the Bible, sometimes call themselves systematic theologies (Paul Tillich's is one example), but though philologically correct (any talk about God, however it is conceived, constitutes theology), this is not the Christian use of the phrase. The Christian idea of theology has always centered upon setting forth the biblical and apostolic Christ, and those (like Tillich) whose theologies do not even attempt to do this would clear the air if they called their productions systematic philosophies of religion instead.

Systematic theology, as was indicated above, is a stockpiling discipline that gathers and combines all the resources of knowledge about God. The six following disciplines draw upon it, interact with and put to work its findings.

5. Apologetics. Apologetics tackles the question, How should we commend and defend the Christian faith, as systematic theology formulates it for us, when we find ourselves confronted by modern unbelief, misbelief, bewilderment and besottedness? What arguments are available to us to justify our faith as reasonable and to build bridges of comprehension and persuasion? Apologetics is almost a department of systematic theology and in fact is often taught as such.

6. Ethics. Ethics asks, What are the ideals and standards of Christian behavior and character? How may we justify them as right, wise, beneficial and fruitful, when we are confronted with criticisms of them (like Nietzsche's, for instance) based on non-Christian views of human nature and destiny? How should we bring biblical principles to bear on particular cases where individuals and communities have to decide what is best to do? Ethics draws its material ultimately from Scripture, but mediately from the accounts of God and man that systematic theology provides.

7. Missiology. Missiology is a relatively new discipline that studies how we should understand and fulfill the ministering tasks on which God sends his people in this world. Cultural anthropology and sociology provide it with necessary knowledge about the world; systematic theology, however, gives it necessary knowledge about human needs as God sees them and about God's strategy for meeting them.

8. Spirituality. Otherwise known as moral, devotional, or ascetic theology, spirituality explores the life of communion with God. Until recently it was subsumed under ethics. It draws material not only from biblical passages that deal with knowing God, opening one's life to him, walking with him, receiving both good and evil (in the sense of Job 2:10 [NIV] "good . . . and . . . trouble") from his hand and being nurtured in grace by him, but also from the digested theological doctrines of God, man and redemption.

9. Liturgy. Liturgy means honorific service, and liturgical study seeks to discern how God is best and most truly worshiped by his people on earth. Worship is essentially a matter of humbly receiving God's gifts and expressing the grateful love that his generosity calls forth. The knowledge of God's goodness in creation, providence and grace that systematic theology provides must therefore give shape to all our worship forms and procedures.

10. Practical theology. Practical theology is an umbrella term covering a wide range of applicatory disciplines. Its question is, How are we to do God's work and glorify his name in our particular serving roles and situations, pastoral, evangelistic, ecclesiastical, administrative or whatever? These are all interface disciplines in which biblical truth about God, man, salvation and Christ's kingdom come together with secular data about the modern world and the people in it. Systematic theology operates here as wholesaler and watchdog, supplying and safeguarding these biblical truths and ensuring that they remain the absolutes to which human ideas are relativized, and not the other way around.

The idea of theology as an elitist enterprise that keeps Christians from taking their Bibles seriously dies hard, but the foregoing analysis will, I hope, help lay it to rest.

The Prejudice Against Theology

My second question grows out of the first. If theology is not obstructive to faith or Bible study, whence came the prejudice against it that I voiced in 1945, and the assumption of its irrelevance that still marks so many believers? These came from the public modeling of theology in the first half of this century.

What happened was this. The antisupernaturalist rationalism that sprang from the deism of the Enlightenment and the pantheism of the Romantic movement had combined with evolutionary euphoria to produce among the professionals a kind of theology that effectively denied the faith of the Bible and the creeds on basics like the Trinity, the incarnation, the atonement, Jesus' miracles, virgin birth, bodily resurrection, ascension and future return as well as the regeneration and conversion of sinners. Theologians holding these "liberal" and "progressive" views, which had temporarily gained establishment status among Protestants, were bland and optimistic about Western culture. But they were also bitter in their contempt for old style Bible-believing faith and energetically undermined it by delineating a pattern of discipleship into which personal conversion did not enter.

This illiberal imperialism on the part of the so-called liberals was declared to be a requirement of theology, and those who stood against it were lambasted unmercifully for being ignorant obscurantists, hopelessly old-fashioned and theologically unaware. Small wonder, then, if the image of theology that crystallized in the thinking of historic Christianity's defenders was of a pernicious, wrong-headed, ideologically structured Trojan horse that Satan's dupes had dragged into the churches to their ruin. People naturally took their idea of theology from watching professed theologians at work, and the steady flow of bad, complacent, antibiblical, culturally captive theology gave theology itself a bad name.

Intellectually, the first half of this century was from every standpoint a bad time for evangelical Christianity. Its resistance to the methods and conclusions of biblical criticism, no matter how erudite and well argued, was held to have destroyed its intellectual credentials. "Critical orthodoxy" based on "the as-sured results of higher criticism" (these were the cant phrases used) wrested denominational and institutional leadership out of evangelical hands through-out the English-speaking world. Thrown on the defensive and marginalized in the thought life of the churches, evangelicals found themselves up the creek without a paddle.

In North America a fundamentalist alliance fought back against the liberal establishment, seeking to make up by ferocity what it lacked in depth and weight of matter; in Britain it was more a case of every one for himself. Wrote the English veteran John Wenham:

> In those days the standard advice given to evangelicals at university was: "Whatever you do, don't read theology." Though based on much painful experience I could see that this policy had no future. It was essential that bad theology should be countered by good theology, so in my third year I took the plunge and read for the Cambridge theology tripos part I. At that time I had been made secretary of what became the Religious and Theological Students' Fellowship (ancestor of UCCF's current Theological Students' Fellowship), and I tried in 1937 to organize our first conference. Evangelical scholarship was at such a low ebb that we could not find a single senior scholar to come and defend the Bible for us.[2]

But the later impact of academics like F. F. Bruce, preachers like D. Martyn Lloyd-Jones, teachers like John Stott and Francis Schaeffer, evangelists like Billy Graham, and institutions like Britain's Tyndale Fellowship and Amer-ica's Fuller Seminary in its early years, turned the situation around partly with a sort of theological renewal following the second World War.[3] Other gifted leaders and significant structures emerged in support of this renewal, not the least of which was the work of cradle liberals like Reinhold Niebuhr and Karl Barth who diligently sabotaged the views in which they had been raised. Today's evangelicals around the world are, on this account, sustained by a theologically literate support structure that is immeasurably stronger than anything that existed fifty years ago.

So it is not surprising to find in evangelical circles distrust of theology as a study and a desire to separate Bible study from it. Suspicion, once aroused, dies hard; the international academic network of theologians is still managed by a liberal rump, and is currently bogged down in mutations of relativism that show continuing failure to believe in revelation and fallen humanity's spiritual blindness in a robustly biblical way. It is clear that the recovery movement in theology has not finished its work yet, and as long as this is so the temptation to zealous Christians to undervalue and abhor theology will remain strong. Perhaps the best antidote is to focus on the models of conservative, nonprofessional, life-oriented, heart-stirring theology provided by such Roman Catholic and Anglo-Catholic laymen as G. K. Chesterton, C. S. Lewis, Charles Williams, T. S. Eliot, Dorothy L. Sayers, Thomas Howard and Peter Kreeft. (I wish I could add some evangelical writers of comparable stature to my list, but I can't and that's that.) The type of theology offered by these writers will most rapidly melt away antitheological prejudice in the hearts of regenerate, Spirit-indwelt Christians who are devoted to God's service and zealous for his honor and glory.

Relating Theology and Bible Reading

What has been said so far has been clearing the ground for the question with which this essay is directly concerned: How do theology and Bible reading relate? The question can now be put, and I shall devote the rest of this essay to making two affirmations that answer it. First, theology as an activity, properly understood, *is* Bible reading as it ought to be, and Bible reading, properly understood, *is* theology as it ought to be. Second, theology as a deposit and a resource can add much to the Bible reading of the individual believer, the study group, the congregation learning together and the wider church.

To the first point, then. It has already become clear that anyone who speaks of God is a theologian in one sense, so that the question is not whether we are going to be theologians but whether we are going to be good ones or bad ones; not clever and elegant as distinct from obtuse and clumsy (much bad theology is clever and elegant), but rather whether we are going to be faithful and biblically accountable as distinct from wayward, fanciful and irresponsible. The question, in other words, is whether we shall theologize (make statements about God) by the light of what the Bible says or by the light of what we like to think.

To be a good theologian one must bow to the authority of Scripture, recognized as the authority of God, and that means learning and laboring to do four things: grasp its message, enthrone its teachings, apply its wisdom and share its truth. But this is precisely the fourfold result to which Bible reading is supposed to lead! Are theology and Bible reading essentially two names for the same thing? Humanly, existentially, religiously—the answer is yes. Theology and Bible reading are one.

Let me state this more fully. Theology is an activity of thought (theologizing) out of which emerge theologies—Calvin's, Augustine's, Wesley's, Barth's, yours and mine. Theology's goal is to know and tell the truth, all the truth we have, about God. That truth embraces the full biblical revelation of God's work, will and ways, centering upon the person and place of Jesus Christ, and the full biblical revelation of what communion with God, worship of God, obedience to God, and the glorifying and pleasing of God, actually involve, both for God's people corporately and for believers individually.

Theology as an activity thus involves four related tasks. First comes the *receptive* task of noting all that is said about what God has done, is doing and intends to do in his lordship over everything and everyone. (That is what I meant by grasping the Bible's message.)

Second comes the *critical* task of relating historic Christian positions and proposals to the biblical witness, both for interpretive help in understanding it and for any corrective adjustments that Scripture may show these positions and proposals to need. (That is what I meant by enthroning the Bible's teaching.)

Third comes the *applicatory* task of drawing from God's revelation of his values, plans and commands practical guidance for our living of contemporary life, plus the parallel exercise of relating revealed truth about the world to what secular philosophy and science say about it. We should note that this latter exercise involves critical cross-questioning ("Does the Bible *really* teach this?"—e.g., Hal Lindsey's view of the future—and "Does empirical data *really* warrant that?"—e.g., an evolutionary origin for the human mind); we should note too that no proposed correlations can be more solid than the biblical and philosophico-scientific reasonings that they bring together are in themselves. (That is what I meant by applying the Bible's wisdom.)

Fourth comes the *communicative* task of finding ways to state what has been learned so as to edify believers, instruct unbelievers, correct distorted notions and rebut anti-Christian arguments. (That is what I meant by sharing the Bible's truth.) Good theology is good Bible reading because it works at these four tasks simultaneously.

So the hydra-headed, ten-disciplined monster called theology that was described earlier turns out to be no more and no less than Bible reading itself, writ large and in good shape. Theology's technicalities (techniques of analysis, specialized vocabulary and so on) are adjuncts of responsible Bible study and should be seen as resources to help us encompass the true and full meaning of Scripture rather than as hindrances that keep us from doing so. The relation is reciprocal, tending, as was said, to identity: Bible reading begets theology, and theology fertilizes Bible reading, and a good specimen of either is also a good specimen of the other. Truly the two are one.

The Deposit of Truth

There is another way of looking at theology that is complementary to the functional account we have just been exploring. This is to see it as the repository (or better still, the deposit itself) of all the truth and wisdom that over the centuries have been found in Scripture, analyzed for coherence, vindicated against skepticism and successfully upheld against alternative understandings.

"Orthodoxy" ("right opinion") is the standard label for this material. To call a belief "orthodox" is to say that its track record historically is of having passed the above tests whenever it was subjected to them, so that now it presents itself to the present-day church and world with altogether credible credentials. Orthodoxy is the content of "doctrine," the theological belief that the church professes and teaches (*doctrina* is Latin for "teaching"). There is a common core of belief that the church has maintained consistently since apostolic days; it is belief in the Creator as Redeemer through the divine-human mediator Jesus Christ, and it is representatively stated in the second century catechetical formula which because of its content (not its authorship) is called the Apostles' Creed.[4]

The main points of this credal orthodoxy are the Trinity (that is, the distinctness of the Father, the Son and the Holy Spirit within the being of God); the Incarnation (that is, the real, virgin-born humanity and the real death, resurrection, ascension, present heavenly reign and future public return of the Son of God who is Jesus); and personal Spirit-wrought salvation (forgiveness of sins, supernatural life in the supernatural fellowship called the church, and the prospect of bodily resurrection and endless glory with God after death). Orthodox theology is a matter of constantly thinking out and passing on these things.

"Doctrine serves four major purposes," writes Alister McGrath. "It aims:

(1) to tell the truth about the way things are; (2) to respond to the self-revelation of God; (3) to address, interpret and transform human experience; (4) to give Christians, as individuals and as a community, a sense of identity and purpose."[5]

Textbooks of theology regularly follow an order of topics that centuries of discussion have shown to be more logical than any other. They lay doctrine out in seven sections, thus: (1) knowing God through his Word and Spirit (a study of method, sometimes called prolegomena in relation to what is to come); (2) God the Creator, triune, sovereign, righteous, loving; (3) humankind, created, fallen and lost; (4) Jesus Christ, the God-man, first humbled then exalted, Lord and Savior, our prophet, priest and king; (5) salvation through the Holy Spirit and new life in Christ; (6) the church, as fellowship and institution; (7) the future, God's and ours (death and Christ's return; resurrection and judgment; heaven and hell). Within this framework fall the historic differences between Protestants, Roman Catholics and Eastern Orthodox. It is important to recognize that these three sorts of Christianity in their classical form have much more in common than divides them, far-reaching though some of their differences are. Yet all three work within this frame, whereas Jews and Muslims and New Agers (for instance) do not.

Christian theological activity (theologizing), then, is essentially a working over of the deposit of theology set out under these headings, and of what is claimed to be wisdom following from it in the fields of apologetics, ethics, spiritual life, worship, mission and pastoral ministry as described above. To study theology is to involve oneself in the task of appropriating, analyzing, evaluating, servicing, and where there is need, reconditioning this heritage of orthodoxy in its application to life.

Why Ordinary Christians Should Be Concerned with Theology

But why should ordinary Christians concern themselves with theology in this sense, "(the) church doctrine," as it is commonly called? Surely we should take our faith and morals from the Bible itself (true); will study of the heritage of Christian orthodoxy help us do that? Can theology actually enrich our Bible reading? When I was eighteen, I thought not, but half a century later I find myself wanting to shout from the housetops, with all the energy and volume I can muster, "Yes, it can!"—in at least the following ways.

1. Theology shows us all how to approach the Bible. A frustrating fact about all forms of verbal communication is stated in the medieval maxim *recipitur ad modum recipientis,* "it is received according to the capacity (brain power and mindset) of the recipient." One thing this means is that we read and hear other people's words through a grid or filter that is created by our own prior interests, preconceptions and emotional involvements or hang-ups. Often we do not "hear" (in the sense of understanding, appreciating or empathizing with) what is said to us on paper or spoken into our ears. Instead we "hear" what we want or fear to hear, giving others' words a spin of significance unrelated to what their utterers had in mind.

A current fashion in literary criticism, deconstructionism, assures us that this is a wonderfully good thing and just as it ought to be. But no ordinary writer, certainly no didactic Christian writer like myself, can agree. Why not? Because we are expressing a meaning of our own which we want people to pick up and hold onto because we think it is *true.* So it is even with the high priests of deconstructionism (who thereby show that they do not take their own contentions seriously), and so it most certainly was with the writers of the Bible. If they knew how today's New Agers, secularists, politicians, irresponsible clergy and bemused laity borrow their phraseology without understanding their meaning, they would turn in their graves. Because the Bible is part of our Western cultural mishmash, a great deal of this goes on, so that even in the churches the question whether there is a "proper" way to read the Bible becomes more and more problematical as each year goes by.

But here theology comes to our rescue. It invites us to try on for size an approach to the Bible that (1) integrates in a coherent way all that the various writers, and with them Jesus Christ, say about the nature of Scripture; (2) squares with all that the Bible writers tell us about God and godliness; and (3) has in essence been followed by the Christian church from the beginning.

The books of the Bible are all books of faith responding one way or another to the realities of divine revelation in history and experience. They are revelation in the sense that by means of this corpus of writings God himself speaks his message to every hearer and every reader, addressing the whole church and the whole world. Scripture is thus God speaking, God preaching and God teaching—God narrating the history of his gracious covenant purpose as he has been working it out in his world through patriarchs, prophets, priests, kings and climactically through Jesus Christ. God models for us in the recorded lives, thoughts and experiences of his servants the way of faith, hope and love, of repentance, endurance, worship, fellowship and good works which he calls us all to take by becoming Jesus' disciples.

Some details of the message may be misunderstood if historical backgrounds are not properly filled in or cultural differences between the Bible times and our own are not properly noted. But the overarching fact is that God and man do not change. Human sin and need on the one hand and divine grace, mercy and supply on the other, remain the same. And the central proclamation, that Jesus Christ saves his people from their sins and so builds God's church, is also (thank God!) forever true. By projecting this orientation to the Bible, an orientation that detailed exegesis consistently confirms in all respects, theology gives us an approach, a viewpoint and a perspective that enable us to see what we are looking at as we travel through the text itself— which leads us to the next point.

2. Theology sets out for us all the substance of the Bible. The Bible is lengthy. It fills over one thousand pages in every English version I know. It is also a very mixed bag. It is a collection of sixty-six books, some of them composites, put together over a period of rather more than a thousand years, and including material of many literary types—prose and poetry, narrative history, celebratory biography and didactic theology; sermons, hymns, letters, statistics, legal and liturgical formulas, a love song, philosophical reflections on the present and visionary anticipations of the future and, as the catalogs say, much, much more. In such a compendium, as in a well-wooded forest, it is easy to lose one's way and wander aimlessly, delighting in all that one sees but never developing any sure sense of direction and never being able to say confidently where one has got to.

Here again, however, theology comes to our rescue, for it offers us time-tested summary statements of that which constitutes the significant core of the biblical message. That Christ is at the center of the Bible is a Christian truism, but it needs to be spelled out. One of the tasks of theology has historically been to do just that. We have already noted how the Apostles' Creed performs this task, giving more space and detail to the saving ministry of Christ and his salvation than to anything else.

When I introduced that Creed I called it a catechetical formula, a text for instructing adult converts. As Alister McGrath puts it:

> The Apostles' Creed had its origins in the early church as a profession or confession of faith made by converts at their baptism. The early church

placed great emphasis upon the importance of the baptism of converts. During the period of Lent (the period from Ash Wednesday to Easter) those who had recently come to faith were given instruction. . . . Finally, when they had mastered the basics of faith, they would recite the Apostles' Creed together, as a corporate witness to the faith . . . which they now understood. . . . These converts would then be baptised with great ceremony and joy on Easter Day itself, as the church celebrated the resurrection of its Lord and Saviour. In this way, the significance of the baptism of the believer could be fully appreciated: he or she had passed from death to life (Rom 6:3-10). . . . A central part of the baptism celebration was the public declaration of faith by each candidate.[6]

Many churches nowadays recite the Apostles' Creed as part of their regular Sunday worship. The rationale for so doing is not fear of heresy in the congregation, but a sense that as part of our praise and homage to God we should recall our baptism and our Christian identity, and focus afresh on the Father's gift of Christ to die for us, on Christ's gift of life and hope to us, and on the Spirit's gift of faith to lay hold of salvation. In grateful celebration we speak out once more the beliefs that mark our passage into the everlasting happiness that is now ours.

McGrath goes on to say:

The creeds provide an outstanding opportunity for wrestling with individual Christian doctrines, and thinking through their importance. In particular, it is helpful to ask the following questions: (1) What scriptural passage does the doctrine integrate? (2) What does it tell us about God? Jesus Christ? ourselves? (3) How can we apply it to our Christian living? (4) How does belief in this doctrine distinguish us from non-Christians? Grappling with the doctrines of the creed is thus an excellent way of deepening our understanding of the Christian faith, and seeing how its various aspects relate.[7]

Exactly! To state the point in the language of this essay, theology in the passive and secondary sense of formulated doctrine (in this case, the catechetical doctrine contained in the Apostles' Creed) stirs us up to practice theology in the active and primary sense of pursuing questions about God that will one way and another strengthen our grip on these Christian basics. By identifying what is essential in biblical faith and positioning us at the most rational starting point for further thought and study, theology in sense two generates theology in sense one.

The generic Christian term for the introductory instruction that brings people to the point where they can say the creed with understanding is *catechism*. This word, together with *catechumen* (a person under instruction) and *catechumenate* (the setup for giving instruction), derives from a Greek word meaning "make to hear." That is what the verb *catechise* essentially means, though the question-and-answer forms of instruction commonly used during the past five centuries have given this word a latter-day significance of grilling people, putting them through their intellectual paces by interrogation. But the thing that makes teaching material catechetical and entitles a course of instruction to be called catechism is the fact that its subject matter is Christian fundamentals as theology defines them, focused throughout on the needs of beginners.

From the fourth century comes a famous set of catechetical lectures by Cyril, Bishop of Jerusalem, addressed to beginner Christians, and the first edition of Calvin's *Institutio Christianae Religionis* (*Institutes of the Christian Religion,* 1536) was a pocket-sized catechetical book addressed to beginner Protestants. Subsequent editions were bulked up so that the book might also function as a higher catechism equipping clergy and ministerial candidates for Bible teaching. In the 1559 preface Calvin states this aim very clearly:

> It has been my purpose in this labor to prepare and instruct candidates in sacred theology for the reading of the divine Word, in order that they may be able both to have easy access to it and to advance in it without stumbling. For I believe I have so embraced the sum of religion in all its parts, and have arranged it in such an order, that if anyone rightly grasps it, it will not be difficult for him to determine what he ought especially to seek in Scripture, and to what end he ought to relate its contents. If, after this road has, as it were, been paved, I shall publish any interpretations of Scripture, I shall always condense them, because I shall have no need to undertake long doctrinal discussions. . . . In this way the godly reader will be spared great annoyance and boredom, provided he approach Scripture armed with a knowledge of the present work.[8]

The knee-jerk reaction of many to this statement might be one of unease. Contemporary evangelicals have been told repeatedly that the Bible should be read humbly and receptively with an open mind, free as far as possible from any form of preconception, so that nothing may hinder the text from interpreting itself to us or hinder us from hearing what it says. Is not Calvin in effect sweeping all that aside and charging us to read Scripture only through his spectacles, forbidding us to find in it anything more than he has already told us is there? Would it not be arrogant, narrowing and enslaving, if as Bible readers and interpreters we were to behave as he recommends? Would it not be Spirit-quenching, so far as interpretation is concerned, to let theology, whether in Calvin's *Institutes* or any other basic book, form our minds before we approach the text?

Not necessarily. Our uneasy fear to the contrary is not so much a mark of spiritual sensitivity and wisdom as it is of antitheological prejudice. Consider what we actually do. When the helps we are offered for our Bible reading take the form of devotional notes or expository outlines or applicatory questions and suggestions or simple commentaries, we receive them gladly and gratefully, using them as handmaids to personal insight. Why then should our hackles go up when the help being offered us is theology—basic catechetical theology, though on the grandest scale (admittedly, Calvin's *Institutes* in its final form is about the length of the Bible itself)?

The truth is that preliminary knowledge is needed when we encounter any aspect of reality; otherwise, quite literally, we look and fail to see. Tour guides round a stately home fulfill their role by pointing out the things one should be looking at, and one of the basic roles of theology in the church is to be a tour guide to the Bible. My wife knows trees, plants and birds very thoroughly in a way that I do not, and so when we walk together in the countryside she sees (recognizes, identifies and appreciates) a great deal more than I do. I would miss these sights entirely if she did not point them out to me. In the same way, people who read the Bible with an overall grasp of its basic teaching will see a great deal more of the implications of each passage and of the wisdom that can be drawn from it, than people who lack such a grasp. To allow theology to prepare us for Bible reading is neither arrogant nor narrowing nor enslaving but enriching, as those who have followed this course can testify.

3. Theology helps us all to maintain the standpoint of the Bible. Theology was presented earlier in this essay as an organism of ten related disciplines, each existing to fulfill a task that somewhere, in some form, the Bible itself imposes on its readers. This ideal description remains valid whether we are thinking of theology as an activity in which we engage or as a heritage centered upon the church doctrine that we have received from the past. Assuming the internal unity and canonical status of the sixty-six books of the Bible (both of which assumptions I believe to be entirely defensible, though this is not the place to defend either), I here make the point that theology conceived in these terms, as a present activity of analyzing, assessing, rethinking and restating the church doctrine under the authority of Scripture, has a critical role to fulfil in relation to the practice of all ten disciplines by their particular exponents, past and present.

By *critical* I mean evaluative. My point is that theology has to proctor and police itself to ensure that by its own criteria it is functioning as right-mindedly as it should. God in his mercy can and often does bless second-rate thinking and performance, using it to bring his people short-term benefits even while it compounds for them long-term problems. But short-term effectiveness does not make the second-rate first-rate, and self-assessment to detect and correct lapses from the standpoint and standards of the written Word of God remains one of theology's constant tasks. *Ecclesia reformata semper reformanda* ("the church that has been reformed always needs to be reformed"—that is, the task of getting the church into better shape is never-ending) is a truth that Reformed churches affirm over and over. Theological assessment and tightening up are basic to the sustained endeavor that the slogan requires.

To preserve a biblical standpoint with regard to biblical faith, three concerns must ever be at the forefront of Christian minds. First, the supremacy of God must be highlighted. That the Creator is the Lord, reigning over his world with unlimited power, unfailing justice and great love, and that he should be worshiped endlessly on this account, is the central emphasis—the center of reference and the center of gravity—throughout the Bible. The twin truths that theology is for doxology and that theology is first and foremost celebration (in narrative and didactic and applicatory forms) of the divine power and goodness is modeled especially in the Psalms. Praise to the God of sovereign grace and gracious sovereignty is integral to the profile of the person whose heart is held steady by true theology. "Great is the LORD, and most worthy of praise . . . Within your temple, O God, we meditate on your unfailing love" (Ps 48:1, 9). "Oh, the depth of the riches of the wisdom and knowledge of God! . . . From him and through him and to him are all things. To him be the glory forever! Amen" (Rom 11:33, 36). "Now to him who is able to do immeasurably more than all we ask or imagine, according to his power that is at work within us, to him be glory in the church and in Christ

Jesus throughout all generations, for ever and ever!" (Eph 3:20).

Living in a human-centered culture with our fallen hearts and heads constantly lapsing into a religiously (or irreligiously) vicious self-absorption, we need the admonitions of theology to keep us facing up to the God-centeredness of the Bible we read. God's sovereignty and supremacy stand out on almost every page of Scripture. Without the ministrations of theology challenging us again and again not to force what we read into an anthropocentric, egocentric mold, we are in danger of missing the life-changing impact of this emphasis and ending up among those whose reading of the Bible never brings them to embrace the Bible's point of view. Such a sad outcome is worth making an effort to avoid. This effort will certainly be blessed by the Holy Spirit. It will be an effort of theology, reminding us and showing us how to read the Bible.

Second, the finality of revealed truth must be upheld. It is a basic biblical conviction that *God* has *spoken,* using his gift to us of language to tell us truth about himself, ourselves and his will for our lives. This is central to Christian faith because it is integrally bound up with belief in the incarnation and the Trinity. If Jesus is divine, then all the words of his teaching were words of God in the most literal sense, including his recognition of his Bible as the authoritative teaching of his heavenly Father (see Mt 4:4, 7, 10; 5:18f.; 9:13; 12:1-7; 15:3-9; 19:2-8, 17-19; 21:13, 16; 22:29-40; Jn 10:35), given through the Holy Spirit (Mt 22:43), much of it referring specifically to him and his vocation as the suffering Messiah (see Mt 5:17; 21:42; 22:41-45; 26:24, 31, 54, 56; cf. 4:13-17; 12:15-21; 21:1-5; Mk 9:11-13; Lk 18:31-33; 22:37; 24:25-27, 45-47; Jn 5:39, 46; 19:28). The church unanimously acknowledged Bible teaching as divinely revealed truth until some two centuries ago. The impossibility of denying it without impugning the incarnation of the Son of God, who has established the principle definitively by his claim to fulfill the Scriptures, was clearly grasped.

But nineteenth century rationalism was hostile to miracles and the supernatural. A variety of factors combined to spread skepticism about revealed truth: the agnosticism that flowed from Kant's influential critical epistemology; the supposed demonstrations by "higher" (source) critics that most Bible history was wrong; and unitarian beliefs about God and nonincarnational views of Jesus that masqueraded among Protestants as enlightened orthodoxy. The concept of propositional revelation, God telling us things, has in our time been decried. We today inherit a situation in which this idea is usually dismissed out of hand.

Theology of a sort has indeed continued. During the past half-century in particular a sense of Christianity being in crisis, under challenge from secularism on one side and ethnic religions on the other, has stimulated a flurry of professional theological work. But where revealed truth has been denied, the work has inevitably been flawed. Some have argued that biblical authority remains a fact even when revealed truth has been dismissed as no more than a fancy. But these arguments fail. Their effect is to reduce Christianity to religiosity—a mixture of mysticism and morality, pious sensibility and ideology. The Bible triggers this off, but without giving us the information that would enable us to distinguish God from human guesses about God. To represent biblical authority in this way, as being functional without being informational, is to turn God into a warm fuzzy who is at the same time an unknown X. This burns the promise of a personal relationship with him to ashes. Denial of the reality of revealed truth thus destroys that knowledge of God to which the Bible invites us. Paul found the Athenians worshiping an unknown God. The knowledge of God offered by much twentieth-century theology is in principle a return to Paul's Athens. We need a theology that receives all Bible teaching as God-given information to guide our steps through the dark mazes of confusion, subjectivist, relativist and sometimes syncretist, which are created for us by theologies that do otherwise.

The strength of theological error is always the truth mixed in with it, and identifying and reclaiming this truth is as much part of the task of engaging it as is detecting its defects. As evil is regularly good gone wrong, so error is regularly truth gone wrong. It must be dealt with accordingly. Blanket acceptance or blanket rejection of positions put to us is easy (and lazy), whereas discriminating assessment is hard work. Theology, as the stockpiled wisdom of the ages regarding which ideas about God are biblical and which are not, is a precious resource for helping us to sort out truth from falsehood and falsehood from truth as we confront today's theological crosscurrents.

Unbiblical theologies (such as liberation theologies) regularly start from biblical texts and claim to be uncovering the authentic thrust of Scripture, so that they have to be evaluated as interpretive hypotheses. Mainstream Christian theology, however, is also a comprehensive interpretive hypothesis, or series of hypotheses. When set alongside the new notions, it will quickly expose their Achilles' heels as attempts to catch the meaning of the Scriptures. Most new notions depend on giving up the finality of God's revealed truth (that is, of all biblical teaching) in some respects. Maintaining the standpoint of the Bible will require a reassertion of this principle, and Christendom's classical theological heritage, which in all its mutations of detail (Protestant, Roman Catholic, Orthodox) is unanimous here, is of great help for this purpose.

Third, the importance of holy living must be understood. Christians inhabiting a world of falling moral standards (as we all do today) easily slip into antinomianism—failure to see that our holy God calls his children to a dedicated, upright life, based on avoiding the sins condemned in the Decalogue and other Scriptures and practicing instead Christlike self-denial, purity, humility and love. As God's revealed truth gives us doctrinal absolutes (because God's knowledge of himself and his ways with mankind do not change), so it gives us ethical absolutes (because God's delight in some ways of behaving and his hatred of other ways does not change either).

The contemporary Christian focus in ethics is on building relationships that express love. Though totally right in itself, this emphasis seems in today's discussions to run the risk of forgetting that holiness involves observing the Bible's ethical absolutes, which belong to God's design for human life. Discussions of sexual ethics—divorce and remarriage, pre- and nonmarital sex, homosexual behavior—are cases in point. The heritage of Christian theology is strong on ethical absolutes and can give us the help we need in focusing the holiness we must pursue, in reliance on the Holy Spirit, if the standpoint of the Bible is to find expression first in our thoughts and then in our lives.

4. Theology forearms us all against heretical understandings of the Bible. This point continues the last. Heresy is ordinarily truth twisted to a shape suggested by the surrounding culture. Our post-Christian culture presses us, in ways of which we are not always conscious, to distort revealed truth by squeezing it into the molds of relativism, pluralism, evolutionism, anthropocentrism, irrationalism, pessimism and various other "isms" of our time. If we read the Bible through the lens of distorting cultural prejudice, it will be misread, just as it will be if we read it with a spirit of reaction or iconoclasm or alienation from the church. And then interpretations that are really heretical (incompatible with established truth) are likely to result. Limits of space forbid proper discussion of this. Suffice it to say that awareness of historic Christian orthodoxy, and of the biblical reasoning that lies behind it, is a timely safeguard against such lapses.

G. K. Chesterton seems to have been right when he observed that it is beyond the wit of man nowadays to invent a new heresy. That makes it all the more important and fruitful to learn to recognize old heresies when they reappear in modern dress. Our Bible reading will certainly benefit if we are able to do this. Heresies within the church, and cults without, regularly appeal to the Bible, read in their own "let's be different" way, to support their own unbiblical positions. But theology will help us find our way through the heretical minefields.

Spiritual Understanding

A century ago advocates of higher criticism frightened laypeople away from personal Bible reading by giving the impression that a great deal of preliminary learning is essential before one can understand the Bible properly. The last thing I want my account of the value of theology to do is to leave any such impressions as that. Introducing the first edition of his collected works in 1547, Luther illustrated from Psalm 119 three things that together make the theologian: prayer (pleading for light), meditation (meaning hard thought), and temptation (in the sense of pressure not to confess and obey the truth one knows). Prayer made, meditation sustained and temptation resisted, will lead to the spiritual understanding that theology exists to safeguard. So said Luther, and he was right.

There can be much spiritual understanding where there is little or no technical theological education. Anyone who reads and rereads the Bible carefully and prayerfully, asking to be taught by God the Holy Spirit about knowing God through our Lord Jesus Christ, will do well; our faithful God will see to that. These pages of mine are simply making the marginal comment that some knowledge of and commitment to theology may well help such a Bible student do even better.

Any who seek an adult foundation-laying in theology will benefit from Bruce Milne, *Know the Truth* (Downers Grove, Ill.: InterVarsity Press, 1982) and James Montgomery Boice, *Foundations of the Christian Faith* (Downers Grove, Ill.: InterVarsity Press, 1986). My own *Knowing God* (Downers Grove, Ill.: InterVarsity Press, 2nd ed. 1993), *Growing in Christ* (Wheaton, Ill.: Crossway Books, 1994) and *Concise Theology* (Wheaton, Ill.: Tyndale House, 1983) might be useful also.

The Sociology of Knowledge & the Art of Suspicion
(A Sociological Interpretation of Interpretation)

Craig M. Gay

I N A BOOK DISCUSSING evangelical hermeneutics, why devote a chapter to a sociological interpretation of interpretation? Don't we have enough to worry about just trying to determine the meaning of the biblical texts without then submitting our findings to yet another level of interpretation? Besides, hasn't the discipline of sociology been used to "debunk" evangelical understandings and undermine Christian orthodoxy? Haven't sociologists consciously sought to replace Christian theology with a purportedly more "rational" interpretation of social reality? Yet in spite of this difficulty, it is important to discuss a few sociological insights in conjunction with evangelical hermeneutics for at least three reasons.

The first is that, in spite of the fact that we may not recognize it, most of us *think* sociologically. This is not to say that sociology has been the most significant influence on our thinking (psychology has probably been more influential), or that our sociological thinking is at all disciplined, or that we are consciously aware of the key issues in social theory, etc. Still, most of us have grown used to thinking about life in general and about our lives in particular from the perspective of how we have been shaped by the societies we live in, and to do this is to think sociologically.

A second reason for including some mention of sociology in this discussion is that the discipline has provided the core insights of a number of very influential recent theological movements. We're going to take a close look at a few of these movements in the following pages. Suffice it here to say that the so-called "theologies of liberation" are by and large sociological theologies in the sense that they see the theological challenge today as one of adjusting Christian belief and practice to the social realities revealed by sociological analysis.

The third, and obviously most important, reason for talking about a sociological interpretation of interpretation is that sociological insights can help us to become better interpreters, inasmuch as some of these insights are true.

Thus far our discussion of hermeneutics has focused almost entirely on the Bible, that is, on that which we are interested in interpreting. We have been encouraged to ask certain questions. What was the historical setting of a particular text? What is its genre? Why did its author say the things he did and in the way he did? How would the text have been understood by its original audience? Why did Israel and/or the church include the text in the canon? How are we to understand the text's meaning today? etc. While these text-centered questions are obviously important to the task of interpretation, a sociological perspective asks us to turn our attention away from the text per se to ask some embarrassing and potentially invidious questions of those who do the interpreting. Setting the text aside, the sociologist turns to the interpreter of the text and asks questions like: Says who? Why should we believe what you're telling us? Whose interests are you protecting? What's in this for you?

Just as the title of this chapter is meant to suggest, a sociological interpretation of interpretation asks that we direct a little healthy suspicion toward all of those who are so anxious to tell us how we ought to read and understand Scripture. It asks that we undertake a little investigative journalism, as it were, in an attempt to find out more about these would-be authorities and to find out what just what kind of stake they might have in their interpretive schemes.

Interestingly, the sociological interpretation of interpretation is anticipated in one of Jesus' encounters with the Pharisees described in Mark's Gospel:

The Pharisees and some of the teachers of the law who had come from Jerusalem gathered around Jesus and saw some of his disciples eating food with hands that were "unclean," that is, unwashed.

So the Pharisees and teachers of the law asked Jesus, "Why don't your disciples live according to the tradition of the elders instead of eating their food with 'unclean' hands?"

He replied, "Isaiah was right when he prophesied about you hypocrites; as it is written:

'These people honor me with their lips,
   but their hearts are far from me.
They worship me in vain;
   their teachings are but rules taught by men.'

You have let go of the commands of God and are holding on to the traditions of men."

And he said to them: "You have a fine way of setting aside the commands of God in order to observe your own traditions! For Moses said, 'Honor you father and mother,' and 'Anyone who curses his father or mother must be put to death.' But you say that if a man says to his father or mother: 'Whatever help you might otherwise have received from me is Corban' (that is, a gift devoted to God), then you no longer let him do anything for his father or mother. Thus you nullify the word of God by your tradition that you have handed down. And you do many things like that." (Mk 7:1-2, 5-13 NIV)

While this terse account makes the Pharisees' mistake appear obvious, we will take a closer look at this passage because the situation was somewhat more complicated than that. The Pharisees apparently considered the taking of oaths, and especially the taking of oaths to God, to be a very serious business. The practice of vowing things to God's service lay at the heart of Israel's highly regulated system of worship. It was something that bound it together and made social interaction orderly and predictable, not unlike the honoring of contracts in our own system. It was held to be axiomatic that the claims of God were to take precedence over the claims of human beings.

This is what was implied by the term *Corban,* which simply meant no merely human claim could interfere with the giving to God of those things that had been vowed to his service. When someone vowed something to God's service, this obligation was held to supersede all other obligations, even caring for parents. Although such a position might seem self-evidently immoral, it was not without solid support from the Torah. Numbers 30:2 states, "When a man makes a vow to the LORD or takes an oath to obligate himself by a pledge, he must not break his word but must do everything he said." Thus what may appear to us now as a blatant distortion of scriptural truth probably represented a genuine moral dilemma for the Pharisees, a dilemma in which service to God unfortunately (and perhaps even tragically) overrode service to human beings.

As the text indicates, however, Jesus sliced through the notion of Corban and indelicately exposed the heart of the matter, that the Pharisees had allowed a commitment to the "traditions of men" to nullify the word of God. It is important to notice why and especially how Jesus did this. Why he did so is relatively obvious. In allowing the notion of Corban to override the fifth commandment, the Pharisees had completely lost sight of the principles that unify the Scriptures—namely, love and mercy—and had adopted instead a rigidly legalistic hermeneutic that allowed people to neglect even their own parents by appealing to their obligations to God. This had the effect of setting the love of God over and against the love of neighbor. But beyond the question of why Jesus condemned the Pharisees in this instance, *how* he did this, at least for the present discussion, is at least as interesting. In the Matthean description of this encounter (Mt 15:1-11) Jesus uses the term *hypocrisy* to describe the Pharisee's hermeneutic.

Originally a theatrical term denoting acting or playing a role, the term *hypocrisy* (Gk *hypokrisis*) by New Testament times had assumed the distinctly negative connotations it still has of dissimulation and acting under false pretenses. What Jesus suggested in using this term, and what the passage from Isaiah actually stated, was that the Pharisees were only *pretending* to honor God with the notion of Corban when in fact their real interests lay elsewhere. Where did these interests lie? Probably in garnering honor and recognition for themselves. Along this line the Gospel writers have a habit of commenting on the Pharisees' love of status and public deference. It is important to notice, however, that the Pharisees did not claim this honor and public recognition directly. These claims were "laundered" through the institution of Israel's religion. The Pharisees were admired, in other words, for being scrupulous servants of God. So well were these claims laundered, in fact, that the Pharisees had themselves become oblivious to their own pretense. We have no reason to doubt that they honestly believed that they were serving God in their traditions. If this service translated into substantial power and privilege, as it almost certainly did, then such were the appropriate rewards for dedication, selflessness and righteousness. It is also important to notice how the notion of Corban fit into the Pharisees' pretense. It protected the flow of resources into Israel's religious system and, by extension, to those responsible for this system.

Our suspicions ought to be aroused at this point, because serving God amounted to a pretty sweet deal for the Pharisees. Our suspicions ought to be further heightened by the fact that the goods vowed to God's service did not actually have to be removed from profane use. They could continue to be used by those who had pledged them. And so the system was such that the Pharisees could, in effect, have their cake and eat it too; they could satisfy the demands of righteousness and their material self-interests at the same time.

In terms of a hermeneutic of suspicion, we might say that the Pharisees had adopted a hermeneutic—plausible in its own right—that protected a system of tradition from which their own power, privilege and prestige were derived, a system *in which they had vital social interests.* As Jesus so bluntly pointed out to them, however, this hermeneutic had the effect of nullifying the word of God both in its letter and in its spirit. While the Pharisees had preserved the appearance of righteousness in the observance of Corban, this observance served as a pretense for furthering their own vested (cleverly hidden) interests, interests which were intricately woven into the fabric of Israel's social and religious system. So well were these interests hidden, in fact, that the Pharisees were undoubtedly genuinely offended at Jesus' charge of hypocrisy. Small wonder that they eventually concluded that protecting Israel's religious system would require Jesus' death.

Before we get too excited about exercising the kind of hermeneutical suspicion just outlined, we need to be reminded, just as Paul reminded the Roman Christians, that we are also "without excuse" in the sense that we are just as likely to read our own interests into Scripture. Indeed, we seem to have a natural propensity to *use* truth, even (and perhaps especially) scriptural truth, to our own advantage. The charge of hypocrisy is thus one that perhaps no one is entirely innocent of. Just as Jesus exposed the hypocrisy of the Pharisees' use of Corban, so we must try to uncover the vested social interests that have become part and parcel of our own reading of Scripture. As responsible interpreters of Scripture, we must subject ourselves to critical suspicion. One very useful tool in this connection is the sociology of knowledge.

Stated simply, the sociology of knowledge is a discipline that attempts to explore the relation between knowledge and its social context—that is, the relation between *what* people think and *who* they are, sociologically speaking. The discipline is organized around the insight that people, acting together in society, produce structures and institutions ("traditions" or "cultures" if you like) which subsequently have an impact on the ways they think about the world and about themselves. The root proposition of the sociology of knowledge, provocatively stated over a century ago by Marx, is that *we create ourselves,* which is to say that in the context of concrete practical material existence we create our own consciousness of reality.

> The production of ideas, of conceptions, of consciousness, is at first directly interwoven with the material activity and the material intercourse of men, the language of real life. Conceiving, thinking, the mental intercourses of men appear at this stage as the direct efflux of their material behavior. The same applies to mental production as expressed in the language of politics, laws, morality, religion, metaphysics of a people. Men are the producers of their conceptions, ideas, etc.—real, active men, as they are conditioned by a definite development of their productive forces and of the intercourse corresponding to these, up to its furthest forms. Consciousness can never be anything else than conscious existence, and the existence of men in their actual life-process.[1]

For Marx, the "material behavior" in the above passage referred to the progressive mastery of man over nature, a mastery summarized in the notion of *praxis,* the manner in which a people responds to the problems of material (read: economic) existence. Due to the dynamic nature of this practical economic process, Marx also insisted that historical development has consistently been plagued by bitter strife. As progressively new praxes have emerged (for example, in a society's transition from an agriculturally based to an industrial economy), violent conflicts have erupted between groups ("classes") with competing practical and material interests. These competing practical and material interests subsequently have surfaced in consciousness as philosophical and/ or religious discord.

While Marx seems to have suggested that human thought simply mirrors competing practical and material interests, subsequent Marxist theorists such as Karl Mannheim argued (following Marx's own teacher, G. W. F. Hegel) that the relation between knowledge (including religious knowledge) and practical material activity is *dialectical,* that is, that new ideas *and* new economic practices have together served to move the historical process forward in an interesting fashion. In a notable study entitled *Ideology and Utopia: An Introduction to the Sociology of Knowledge,*[2] Mannheim suggested that those benefiting from the existing (and by definition "passing") state of affairs have commonly sought—albeit unconsciously—to legitimate and preserve the existing status quo by means of "ideology." Similar to hypocrisy, an ideology is a mode of thought that misrepresents and misunderstands the conditions of its own origin. The nature of misrepresentation is disclosed in that an ideology attempts to secure eternal legitimacy for what are simply temporal and conventional social arrangements, and in that its proponents fail to see that their ideology benefits them vastly more than others in their society. Returning to our earlier example, the Pharisees' use of the concept of Corban appears to have been ideological insofar as it was used to give a kind of divine sanction to the protection of their own vested institutional interests and positions.

Mannheim also observed that those oppressed by the existing status quo have tended to generate "utopian" thought, systems of thought that reach entirely beyond the existing social system toward a future in which things will be brighter for them. In the neo-Marxian analytical tradition, historical social change has thus been interpreted in terms of the ongoing conflict between the advocates of utopian thought and their ideological opponents, a conflict in which ideology is painfully but regularly bested. Put somewhat differently, human existence in the context of the continuous struggle with material scarcity has exhibited the repeated transcendence of utopian visions, generated by the poor and oppressed, over and against the inhibiting influence of ideologies perpetrated by those in positions of power and privilege.

From a neo-Marxian perspective, then, history is viewed primarily in terms of conflict between those in positions of power within the existing socioeconomic order and those oppressed by that order. The neo-Marxian vision suggests that those oppressed within the existing social order have, precisely because they are oppressed, a special ability to understand what truth is and therefore to apprehend where history is going. The poor and oppressed, in other words, are held to possess a kind of epistemological privilege with respect to historical development, and their vision of the future, as it has not yet come into being, cannot be judged by existing morality or by notions of what is realistic at present. Conversely, those in positions of power and privilege within the existing social order are held to be epistemologically handicapped. Because they have vested interests in the present status quo, those currently in positions of power and privilege are at odds with the historical process and are therefore unable to make true judgments about society and historical development.

The critical task of the sociology of knowledge in the Marxian analytical tradition has thus been to correctly identify the major players in the existing social order and to determine *who is being oppressed by whom,* thereby ascertaining where history is going. Recently a great deal of attention has been given to three distinct axes of oppression: political-economic oppression, racist oppression and sexist oppression. The hermeneutical task in the context of these kinds of oppression (whether with respect to political culture, economics, art, modern literature, Scripture or some other realm) has been aimed both at debunking the ideological nature of prevailing interpretations of social reality, and at formulating new, and in a sense utopian, interpretations that attach to the epistemological privilege of the oppressed, thereby purportedly aiding them in their struggle against oppression and presumably moving the historical process forward.

If any of this sounds familiar, it is probably because these insights have been incorporated into a number of recent theological movements all having to do with liberation from oppression. The proponents of these theologies have consciously sought to employ sociology of knowledge analysis in an effort to expose ideological hypocrisy and to restate the meaning of the gospel more faithfully in the context of contemporary oppression. Latin American liberation theology, for instance, has sought to restate the meaning of the gospel in the context of oppressive economic neocolonialism and dependency in the Third World. In North America, a black theology has been developed in the context of white racist oppression and has sought to reinterpret the gospel from the perspective of blackness. The feminist movement has given rise to a distinctive feminist theology in which women have sought to free the gospel from the oppressive influences of sexism and patriarchal domination.

All of these theologies focus on conflicts that are believed to lie at the heart of social existence. All are committed to the notion that conflict between the oppressed and their oppressors is the engine of historical development. It is for this reason that the various theologies of liberation insist that theological thinking, including the interpretation of Scripture, must be preceded by detailed sociological analysis aimed at exposing the actual mechanisms of oppression in any given situation. For Latin American liberation theologians this has meant that theological reflection must spring out of a neo-Marxist analysis of global capitalist oppression. For black theologians it has meant that theology cannot proceed apart from the social and historical analysis of the experience of American blacks. Feminist theologians hold that theology depends on historical and sociological investigations into the nature of patriarchy and gender repression.

In spite of their differences with respect to the nature of oppression, the various theologians of liberation are united in suspecting that the established churches have been ideological allies of the oppressing classes and therefore that the dominant systems of biblical interpretation are ideologically tainted and not to be trusted. Latin American theologian José Míguez Bonino has written:

> It is a crisis of conscience when Christians discover that their churches have become the ideological allies of foreign and national forces that keep the countries in dependence and the people in slavery and need. . . . [But such a realization] opens the door for a new search—the quest for a post-colonial and a post-neo-colonial understanding of the Christian gospel.[3]

Continuing along this line, theologians of liberation have argued that biblical interpretation desperately needs to be liberated from ideological captivity. Feminist theologian Letty Russell has written that "the Bible can become a liberating word for those who hear and act in faith." But "this same message also needs to be liberated from sexist interpretations which continue to dominate our thoughts and actions."[4]

Crucial to the liberation of Scripture from ideological captivity is the realization that interpretation must begin with the *experience* of oppression. Indeed, the message of Scripture is revealed and its authority is instantiated only for those who have experienced oppression. As suggested in the term *epistemological privilege,* the experience of oppression is held to be requisite for understanding truth *as such.* While the theologians of liberation are aware that this represents something of a departure from "established" doctrine, they insist that it has, in fact, been the establishment's abstraction *from* experience that has lain at the root of a great deal of theological evil. This is because truth *must* be experienced to be appreciated and recognized. We are able to recognize the truths embedded in Scripture only to the extent that we have already experienced them. As black theologian James Cone argued in *A Black Theology of Liberation,* black experience (in the sense of the experience of oppression) must be seen as the "primary datum of reality" against which all interpretive projects are measured. Indeed, theologians of liberation contend that attempts to ground interpretation in anything but experience must lead not simply to a loss of theological relevance but ultimately to a complete loss of theological integrity.

The experience of oppression is so central to the theologies of liberation that it is considered revelatory in and of itself. "God's revelation," Cone has written, "comes to us in and through the cultural situation of the oppressed." A prominent feminist theologian has noted similarly,

> By women's experience as a key to hermeneutics or theory of interpretation, we mean precisely that experience which arises when women become critically aware of these falsifying and alienating experiences imposed upon them as women by a male-dominated culture. Women's experience, in this sense, is itself a grace event, an infusion of liberating empowerment from beyond the patriarchal cultural context, which allows them to critique and stand out against these androcentric interpretations of who and what they are.[5]

As implied in the moniker "liberation" theology, the theologies of liberation understand the gospel message to be one of liberation from the oppressive social and economic forces they identify in their respective analyses. As Cone has noted,

> Revelation is God's self-disclosure to humankind in the context of liberation. To know God is to know God's work of liberation on behalf of the oppressed. God's revelation means liberation, an emancipation from death-dealing political, economic, and social structures of society. This is the essence of biblical revelation.[6]

The principal hermeneutical task in the theologies of liberation is to render the biblical texts relevant and useful in the ongoing struggle to liberate the oppressed. Indeed, the acid test of whether or not a passage is revelatory and authoritative has become the question of how well it serves—or fails to serve—the movement toward sociocultural liberation. Cone has insisted, for example, that "any message that is not related to the liberation of the poor in a society is not Christ's message. Any theology that is indifferent to the theme of liberation is not Christian theology."[7] Similarly, feminist theologian Elisabeth Schüssler Fiorenza has argued that "feminist theology must first of all denounce all texts and traditions that perpetrate and legitimate oppressive patriarchal structures and ideologies."[8]

The premium that theologians of liberation place upon the relevance and usefulness of theology in the contemporary social struggle has led them to be highly suspicious of theologies and systems of interpretation which cannot be made to speak more or less directly to the contemporary sociopolitical struggle. All such "conservative" theologies merely obfuscate the real sociohistorical situation and abet the existing status quo by directing attention away from the crucial social task at hand. This explains some of the difficulty theologians of liberation have had with historic Christian orthodoxy and with all hermeneutical traditions which refuse to collapse theology into prophecy for political-social change. Indeed, it is precisely *from* doctrinal orthodoxy, and *from* any suggestion that the gospel might transcend all particular social contexts, that theology needs now to be liberated. The protest against orthodoxy is nicely summarized in the repeated insistence that orthodoxy needs to be replaced with *orthopraxy,* a kind of Christian practice that will be judged only on the basis of how well it contributes to the ongoing sociopolitical task of liberating the oppressed and disabling their oppressors.

Those who object to the theologies of liberation are immediately suspected of ideological collaboration with the existing status quo, and whatever objections they might raise are discounted accordingly. As indicated above, the various theologies of liberation begin by insisting that a kind of epistemological privilege attaches to the victims of oppression and that these victims possess special insight into society and history. To find fault with this insight is to be in error *by definition* and is an unmistakable indication of ideological captivity.

This is not necessarily to say that those who would otherwise be considered oppressors—North Americans, members of the middle class, whites, men and so forth—cannot know truth at all. The theologians of liberation do suggest that even oppressors can possess true insights if they appropriately "identify" with the victims of oppression by adopting the correct sociopolitical outlook. Yet it is important to note that the theologians of liberation are not entirely in agreement on this point. As one might expect, the notion of identification poses particularly difficult problems for black and feminist theologies which attach epistemological privilege to race and gender. Cone has gone as far as to say that it is "unthinkable that oppressors could identify with oppressed existence and thus say something relevant about God's liberation of the oppressed."[9] Less extremely, feminist theologian Rosemary Radford Ruether has written,

> Key to [the] ideological deformation is the movement of the socioreligious group addressed from powerlessness to power. When religious spokespersons identify themselves as members and advocates of the poor, then the critical-prophetic language rediscovers its cutting edge. When religious spokespersons see themselves as primarily stabilizing the existing social order and justifying its power structure, then prophetic language becomes deformed in the interests of the status quo.[10]

Returning to Jesus' criticism of the Pharisees, we might say that the theologians of liberation are attempting to level a similar kind of criticism against all theologies—evangelical or otherwise—which are not sufficiently concerned for the plight of the poor and oppressed. They are saying that the "traditions of men," in this case the sociopolitical mechanisms of oppression by class, race, sex and so on, have ensnared the established (read: comfortable) churches and have led them to effectively nullify or at least blunt the liberating word of God in the world. The gospel of Christ, these theologians insist, is a message of liberation, of *real* liberation to be experienced by *real* people here and now and not simply by disembodied souls in an afterlife. To the extent that the established churches have not been engaged in the struggle to realize this kind of liberation, they have not been agents of the gospel. "Such a church honors Christ with its theology," the theologians of liberation might be imagined to paraphrase Isaiah, "but its *praxis,* and thus its heart, is far from him."

Of course, the theologians of liberation are correct. The gospel *has* been used to defend repressive socioeconomic institutions and policies, and it *has* been used in this way by those who have stood to gain the most from them. Think of the conservative defense of chattel slavery in the American South just a little over a century ago, or of the conservative Christian defense of the policies of apartheid in South Africa more recently. Or think of the enthusiasm with which so many middle-class Christians endorse capitalism as *the* Christian economic system. Leaving aside questions of the relative merits of the market economy, isn't it a little suspicious that the gospel of Jesus Christ has been turned into a gospel of "health and wealth" by the most relatively healthy and wealthy group of people who have ever lived? The myth of a "Christian America" might be mentioned in this connection as well. The doctrine of divine providence notwithstanding, there are good theological and sociological grounds for suspecting that anytime a particular people—especially an affluent and powerful people—claim to stand in a privileged relationship to God, the claim is probably hypocritical and ideological. Certainly the theologians of liberation are onto *something* when they speak about the relative inability of the privileged and powerful to understand the gospel message.

Unfortunately the theologians of liberation do not expose contemporary hypocrisy by directing us back to the text of Scripture, as Jesus did in his confrontation with the Pharisees. While the theologians of liberation do cite Scripture, their final appeal, as discussed above, is to a particular kind of *experience,* namely, the experience of oppression. For them the experience of oppression replaces both Scripture and the church as the norm for faith and life. Indeed, Scripture and the church are themselves judged on the basis of how well (or poorly) they conform to this normative experience. But this begs an obvious question: *whose* experience of oppression ought to serve as the final norm? As we have seen, different theologies of liberation focus on quite different types of oppression and call for quite different kinds of remedies. While the various theologies of liberation share a common enemy in theologically and culturally conservative orthodoxy, it is not difficult to see that these movements must eventually founder on the question of authority. It is easy to imagine them dissolving in a kind of endless regress in which increasingly shrill voices will wrangle over questions like, Who is *really* oppressing whom? What kind of oppression is *really* the worst? Who is *really* the most oppressed?

The other problem with making a particular kind of experience normative for theology is that it tends to lead to a kind of hermeneutical ventriloquism in which the Bible is made to appear to say things that have obviously been arrived at along extrabiblical lines. But the moral and rhetorical force of the theologies of liberation derives from their claim to biblical authenticity. So the more obvious this ventriloquism is, the less convincing these theologies become. For these theologies to be seen as too traditionally biblical, on the other hand, would threaten important alliances they have established with secular movements of liberation which view traditional religion with suspicion.

Theologians of liberation have thus found themselves caught between two mutually exclusive constituencies. On the one hand, they need to convince the church that their positions are genuinely biblical. They also need to convince their secular counterparts that their positions are not so biblical as to identify them as enemies of historical social change. Needless to say, this is a difficult position to be in. While the various theologies of liberation have enjoyed the intellectual limelight of late, the future does not look so bright for them.

In spite of these difficulties, theologians of liberation are nothing if not committed to the cause of progressive sociohistorical liberation. Indeed, their commitment to progress is such that it supersedes *all* other commitments, including the commitment to assess historical and social realities with any degree of objectivity. Along this line, one senses that no *actual* change in social reality—for example, no *actual* alleviation of oppression—would lead these theologians either to doubt or to abandon their social and historical programs; and in this sense the theologies of liberation really are "utopian." Black and feminist theologies are insulated from historical failure to some extent because race and sex/gender are social constants, but it will be interesting to see what impact, if any, the former Soviet Union's recent movement in the direction of a market economy will have on Latin American liberation theology. While the recent revolution in Eastern Europe would seem to call for a fairly substantial overhaul of the neo-Marxist foundations upon which Latin American liberation theology has been constructed, it would not be too surprising to see these theologies carry on as if nothing had happened. Praxis, it seems, is no real match for theory after all.

The strength of liberation theology's commitment to a particular understanding of the world and history, even in the face of a good deal of counterfactual evidence, raises an interesting question for the sociology of knowledge, a question that needs to be answered if our discussion is to move forward. Just as we have seen that it is possible for materially vested interests to distort our reading of Scripture, couldn't our understanding of Scripture be similarly distorted by prior commitments to particular visions or understandings of reality? Put somewhat differently, Is the abuse of Scripture always and only a function of vested material interests—power, privilege, comfort, etc.—or can this abuse also stem from vested interests in *ideas?* Could not a commitment to a particular understanding of reality (the term "controlling myth" has been used in this connection) be potentially even more problematic than vested material interests when it comes to interpreting Scripture? The answer to these questions is yes. The reason for answering them in the affirmative is simply that we do not live by bread alone. We also live by *meaning* and by trying to *make sense* of our world and of our lives and purposes in this world. To use a term that has become popular of late, we need a paradigm for understanding and interpreting our experience. And we need to construct this paradigm *in society with others*. The interpretive paradigm that we construct together with others serves to unite us in communities of purpose and meaning outside of which we would find it difficult to live at all. Our hunger for a community of meaning and purpose often far exceeds our hunger for purely material things. This is particularly true in a context of generalized affluence and leisure. Once basic material needs have been met, the need for meaning and purpose becomes especially acute. As sociologist Robert Nisbet warned some years ago, this need quickly becomes subject to manipulation:

> Contemporary prophets of the totalitarian community seek, with all the techniques of modern science at their disposal, to transmute popular cravings for community into a millennial sense of participation in heavenly power on earth. When suffused by popular spiritual devotions, the political party becomes more than a party. It becomes a moral community of almost religious intensity, a deeply evocative symbol of collective, redemptive purpose, a passion that implicates every element of belief and behavior in the individual's existence.[11]

Sixties radicals Peter Collier and David Horowitz have provided a powerful second to Nisbet's observations recently in a book of reflections on their involvement in the New Left:

> Not an intention but a totalitarian *faith* is what creates the common bond between . . . progressive believers. . . . Totalitarianism is the possession of reality by a political Idea—the Idea of the socialist [or black or feminist, etc.] kingdom of heaven on earth, the redemption of humanity by political force. To radical believers, this Idea is so beautiful it is like God Himself. It provides the meaning of a radical life. It is the solution that makes everything possible; it is the end that justifies every regrettable means. Belief in the kingdom of socialist heaven is the faith that transforms vice into virtue, lies into truth, evil into good. For in the revolutionary religion,

the Way, the Truth, and the Life of salvation lie not with God above but with men below—ruthless, brutal, venal men—on whom the faith confers the powers of gods. There is no mystery in the transformation of the socialist paradise into Communist hell: Liberation theology is a Satanic creed.[12]

Collier and Horowitz may overstate their point, but the theologians of liberation have indeed constructed a community of meaning of purpose based on something like the following tenets. The first may be summarized as an Enlightenment faith in historical human progress, or the notion that just and good social and political community lie within our grasp if only we exert the moral and intellectual will to effect them. This commitment to progress is wedded to the gnostic epistemology we discussed above which suggests that only certain kinds of persons (those who espouse the correct social and political opinions) are really able to understand the present historical moment and therefore ultimately to apprehend truth itself. Not surprisingly, this potent combination has led to rather radical suspicion, not simply of the past, but of all understandings which refuse to reduce the sum total of human aspirations to political-social change. Historic Christian orthodoxy scores poorly on this test because it has stubbornly refused to collapse the kingdom of God into merely human history and culture. Returning to our point about vested ideal interests, if we admit that prior commitments to ideas can have the effect of distorting our understanding of Scripture, then the theologies of liberation provide a fairly obvious example of just this kind of distortion, for by their own admission the kinds of commitments just outlined decisively shape their understanding and use of Scripture.

In spite of their claims to be radical, then, we might say that the theologies of liberation have not really been radical enough, either theologically or sociologically. They have not been radical enough theologically because they have failed to realize that from the perspective of the gospel, death and powerlessness are ultimately the only remedies for abusive authority and oppression. They fail to come to grips with the theology of the cross. There is nothing particularly new in this kind of failure. The theologians of liberation only repeat the mistake the crowd made when it chose to have Pilate release a political insurrectionist rather than Jesus. Yet it is important to stress that the various theologies of liberation are not radical enough sociologically either. This is because they do not succeed (indeed, do not even seem interested) in liberating hermeneutics from particular communities of meaning and purpose. While theologies of liberation correctly identify the kinds of distortions material interests introduce into biblical interpretation, they completely neglect the distortions that stem from vested ideal interests. They fail to see how insidiously biblical interpretation may be corrupted by prior commitments to particular theories about the nature of social reality. Perhaps this is because they consider their own communities of meaning and purpose to be revelatory in and of themselves.

If the theologies of liberation have not been radical enough, perhaps it is because they have not yet fully apprehended the variety of ways that knowledge is shaped and constrained by social forces. As Marx suggested, knowledge is constrained by the material and economic struggle for survival, that is, within the "actual life process" as he put it; but as we have seen, knowledge is also constrained by our need to understand and to make sense of our world and by the commitments we make to communities of meaning and purpose. In fact, these latter considerations have led a number of theorists to speak of *the social construction of reality itself* and to propose an even broader conception of the sociology of knowledge than the one we have been working with thus far.

Although the suggestion that reality is socially constructed may at first glance appear to be self-evidently preposterous, we need to consider this proposition more closely. It is not as absurd as it sounds. What this does *not* mean is that we create nature and our own existence *as such,* for such a suggestion would be absurd indeed. What the social construction of reality does imply, however, is that we do create a social reality for each other and that this social reality shapes our consciousness of ourselves and of the world. In the course of acting together in society with others, if we define something as "real," then this definition will have real consequences for us. Language is perhaps the most obvious example of this. Language is obviously a human product, and yet it circumscribes the boundaries of our ability to think about and experience reality. Take the example of the caveat just cited above—that we do not socially construct nature and existence as such. Perhaps not. But the concepts "nature" and "existence" are social constructs, and our actual experience of whatever it is these words signify is shaped by them. One example of this is given in the often-cited observation that Eskimos have a large number of different words for "snow," which is understandable given the amount of snow they must contend with. What this means, in effect, is that their experience of snow is richer and more nuanced than ours. Similar observations have been made about verbs as well as nouns. Certain Greek tenses, for example, describe types of actions for which there is no English equivalent. For English speakers, these kinds of actions do not, in a sense, exist because we do not possess the verb tenses to describe them. Obviously much more could be said about the mystery of language, but let it suffice here to say that it seems to provide a kind of archetypal example of the social construction of reality.

The social construction of reality is a communal affair. Our understanding of reality is maintained by those we live and associate with in communities of meaning and purpose. It is important to recognize that the social realities we construct for ourselves do not necessarily have to line up neatly with reality per se. Indeed, much of human history might be described as one long succession of more-or-less successful (albeit futile) attempts to ignore the realities of creation, Torah and God. Returning to the Pharisees, perhaps their chief problem lay in their construction of a religious reality that precluded the kind of messiah that Jesus turned out to be. While it is undoubtedly true to say that the Pharisees profited materially from this arrangement, this does not begin to tell the whole story, for they must also have profited ideally as well. This is because the religious system they had constructed (the "traditions of men," as Jesus put it, quoting Isaiah) was eminently well-suited to satisfy the natural human desire to be justified before God on the basis of human accomplishments. Following the apostle Paul, we might say that the religious system the Pharisees had constructed (including humanly constructed religious systems in general) show a natural inclination toward idolatry and "the works of the law," inclinations which make it very difficult for us to recognize the reality of grace.

The tenacity of our commitment to socially constructed religious realities is demonstrated in the energy with which the various theologies of liberation have been advocated in recent years. As indicated above, these theologies have constructed a social reality that is defined by a particular reading of historical social change. But we need to ask two questions about this constructed reality. The first is whether or not we can establish any links between the social location of the advocates of this reality and the ideas that make it up. For example, we might point out that the theologies of liberation, in spite of their rhetoric about the epistemological privilege of "the poor and oppressed," still require an epistemological or intellectual elite to interpret and systematize the otherwise disorganized insights of the oppressed masses. The proponents of liberation theology, for the most part highly educated intellectuals, stand ready to serve the masses by stepping into this role. The question to ask here is simply, Is this a coincidence? Perhaps it is; but we would do well to be suspicious of intellectuals who devise interpretive systems in which essentially all social and political power accrues to themselves.

An interesting example of the insidious effect that vested material and ideal interests can have on biblical interpretation is given in the recent debate over capitalism, a debate that has proven quite divisive within North American evangelicalism in recent decades. The evangelical debate has taken place against the backdrop of a kind of cultural war between an old, or traditional, segment of the middle class generally associated with the production and distribution of material goods and a new segment of the middle class associated with the production and distribution of knowledge and information. While space does not permit a detailed analysis of this conflict, suffice it to say that each segment tends to champion by way of a variety of ideologies those things that it does best. Members of the old middle class, for example, typically defend capitalism and business enterprise and advocate market solutions to social problems. They are suspicious of intellectuals and government bureaucrats. Members of the new class, on the other hand, tend to be quite critical of capitalism and suspicious of business interests and would much rather see political and social authority vested in universities and planning agencies, those places where they happen to be employed.

Evangelicals have, in effect, acted as chaplains to both sides in this conflict. Some evangelicals have become conscious advocates of the social and political agenda of the new class and have therefore become quite critical of capitalism and business interests. Others have chosen to voice the interests of the old or traditional middle class and have become very defensive of capitalism and very critical of the knowledge elite. Both groups have made very direct appeals to Scripture (albeit to different parts of Scripture) to make what are essentially antithetical cases.

But we probably do well to be suspicious of all those who are either *very* critical or *very* defensive of capitalism, especially if this criticism or defense appears to be derived from Scripture. Both positions signal ideological advocacy on either side of a social and cultural conflict.

To make these sorts of sociological arguments is not to suggest that our ideas and beliefs are somehow socially determined and thus nothing but the reflection of such factors as class membership. People are much more complicated and unpredictable than that. Indeed, the notion of personal responsibility implies freedom with respect to just these kinds of sociological determinants. In addition, sociological observations should *not* be taken to imply insincerity on the part of those involved in social conflicts, for there is little reason to doubt that advocates on either side of most conflicts honestly believe in the merits of their respective cases. What this sociological discussion does mean, however, is that people tend to be attracted to ideas and conceptions with which they have an affinity and that they tend to ignore or discount other ideas and conceptions with which they do not have such an affinity. This is why the ideological abuse of knowledge is often not so much a matter of the direct corruption of knowledge as it is a matter of handling knowledge *selectively*. Such selectivity obviously has a bearing on biblical interpretation.

A second set of questions we might want to ask about the theologies of liberation is, Why have these theologies, which obviously represent a rather significant departure from historic Christian orthodoxy, become popular of late? What explains their current *plausibility?* Addressing the first question, liberation theology's commitment to historical progress is eminently plausible in the context of a world that has been completely transformed in recent centuries, both at the level of institutions and at the level of consciousness, by the processes of modernization. The progress we have already witnessed in the areas of production, transportation, consumption, communications and the like is such that it is not entirely unreasonable to imagine that society might actually be more or less perfectible with continued progress. In a similar vein, the rapid expansion of human technical skill in recent centuries and the explosion of human knowledge generally have made it plausible for us to believe that history really is a human project and that humanity really has "come of age," so to speak. The modern political apparatus has experienced such unprecedented growth in the past century that it is no wonder that the theologies of liberation would put such a strong, and occasionally exclusive, emphasis on the political relevance of the gospel.

The theologies of liberation may also be said to make sense in the context of modern secularity. While there are a variety of interesting reasons for the secular quality of modern social and cultural life, one curious effect of this secularity is that it has left highly educated persons in the difficult position of being simultaneously alienated from traditional religious interpretations of reality and acutely hungry for the very communities of meaning and purpose that religion was once able to provide. In this context, the theologies of liberation (which are, for the most part, secularized versions of traditional Christianity) appear understandably attractive. While these theologies retain the language and structure of Christian orthodoxy, they translate this language and structure in such a way that God's agency is collapsed into our own, thereby affirming that history and social change are primarily human projects. Although the theologies of liberation would probably have been quite incredible prior to the onset of modernization (and probably still are in many parts of the world today), certain features of modern society have rendered them increasingly attractive to modern intellectuals.

This is not to suggest that the theologies of liberation are nothing but reflections of the process of modernization, and it is not to suggest that these theologies are not advocated sincerely. Still, the sociologist of knowledge cannot help but wonder why these theologies, or any other theological movement for that matter, have arisen and have become so popular at this particular historical juncture.

In using the sociology of knowledge to investigate the theologies of liberation, we turn the tables on them, in a sense. Just as they have accused the established church of ideological collaboration with various systems of oppression, so we have accused them of a kind of cultural captivity, one that their conflict-centered model of social reality apparently prevents them from seeing. We have relativized the relativizers.

Before we congratulate ourselves on this clever intellectual feat, however, we need to realize that we have paid a high price to do this. We have, in effect, admitted that knowledge, even religious knowledge, is situationally relative and can be interpreted in terms of its social location. This admission is so pricey because we cannot exempt ourselves from it. If we are going to apply the analytical scalpel of the sociology of knowledge to the arguments of our opponents, not only can we can expect the favor to be returned, but we can also expect to become suspicious of ourselves and so to experience potentially painful self-doubt. We will be led to suspect that if our own beliefs were subjected to a sociology of knowledge analysis, they might not test entirely free of ideological bias. We are historically and socially situated, and we cannot help but be involved and implicated in the historical currents and social conflicts of our time. The benefits that accrue to us from the use of sociology of knowledge come at the cost of having to admit that truth is, at least as far as we are concerned, situational and relative.

Several things take the edge off this difficult admission that our grasp of truth is situational and relative, however. The first is simply the existence of science, which indicates that it is possible in principle to transcend our particular circumstances and to know certain things about the world around us. Even the fact that we can point in retrospect to the specific sociological and/or psychological factors that led to scientific discoveries does not completely debunk the truthfulness of these discoveries. As sociologist Peter Berger has noted:

> The case of mathematics is rather instructive in this connection. Without any doubt mathematics is a projection onto reality of certain structures of human consciousness. Yet the most amazing fact about modern science is that these structures have turned out to correspond to something "out there" (to quote the good Bishop Robinson). Mathematicians, physical scientists, and philosophers of science are still trying hard to understand just how this is possible. What is more, it is possible to show sociologically that the development of these projections in the history of modern thought has its origins in very specific infrastructures without which the development is most unlikely ever to have taken place. So far nobody has suggested that *therefore* modern science is to be regarded as a great illusion. The parallel with the case of religion, of course, is not perfect, but it is worth reflecting upon.[13]

In the years since Berger made these observations a number of people *have* suggested that modern science is nothing but an ideological tool of those in positions of power. But most reasonable people take the existence of science to mean that it is possible in principle to make true statements about the world. And if it is possible to make true statements about the world, then it would seem that we ought to be able to make true statements about our participation in the world. If it is possible for us to say true things about our participation in the world, then we ought in principle to be able to say true things about the nature of the God whose world this is and in whose image we have been created, just as the apostle Paul argues in Romans. But this is to jump ahead of the argument. The point here is simply that the existence of science indicates that, in spite of the fact that our "reality" is socially constructed, our constructed social reality is constrained and disciplined by reality *as such*. It would be impossible, for example, to construct a viable social reality in which friendship had nothing to do with fidelity, or in which children no longer required loving nurture of parents, or in which people were not permitted to seek and perhaps find God.

The second observation that helps take the edge off our confession that our grasp of truth is situational and relative, is that it is possible for us to transcend our own biases by way of disciplined self-criticism. Indeed, the point of this entire chapter is to suggest that it is possible for us—through the sociology of knowledge—to recognize and anticipate the kinds of ideological biases that we are subject to so that we can avoid becoming completely blinded by them.

While space does not permit a detailed discussion of the methodology of the sociology of knowledge here (experts are divided on the question anyway), several commonsense points can be mentioned. The first is that while the sociology of knowledge provides us with a useful perspective for self-examination, it is a fairly blunt instrument. This is because the social phenomena to which the sociology of knowledge perspective is most sensitive—class conflicts, social processes, generalized social trends and so on—tend to be rather large in scale. In addition, and as indicated above, the ideological abuse of truth often tends to be more a matter of selectivity than of outright falsification. For this reason the sociology of knowledge perspective is most usefully applied to interpretive schemes in which it is possible to determine patterns of inclusion and exclusion. The sociology of knowledge perspective is also most usefully applied in situations of conflict where one group's selection of facts and interpretations can be compared with that of other groups with competing social interests. In the case of biblical interpretation, the sociology of knowledge will perhaps be most applied to the questions of social ethics.

In regard to the methodology of the sociology of knowledge, and at the risk of oversimplification (here again the experts are divided), the sociology of knowledge approach can be said to consist of three stages. The first stage is descriptive. We simply want to make sure that we understand the knowledge in question—whether a particular system of interpretation of Scripture, a particular public-policy stance, a treatise on social ethics or something else— as thoroughly as possible. We want to be sure that we understand the argument not simply as stated, but also in terms of what the argument assumes and takes for granted. What kinds of empirical assumptions (that is, about the existing state of affairs) does the position make? What kinds of normative assumptions does the argument make about why the existing state of affairs matters, and what we should do about it? In sum, we want to understand what kind of social reality the position presupposes and attempts to address.

The second stage of a sociology of knowledge analysis is also descriptive but focuses on *who,* sociologically speaking, these subjects are instead of on what the subjects of our investigation are saying. How, for example, do they make a living? What position do they occupy in the larger social order? We are interested in discovering the extent to which our subjects are members of groups that have discernible social interests, for this may help to explain why our subjects may have adopted the particular positions they have, and why they may have neglected and/or ignored certain other alternatives.

The third stage in a sociology of knowledge analysis involves trying to link the knowledge in question with the social location of the people who espouse it. This is obviously the most important stage of analysis, but it is also the most problematic. This is because even if such a link can be plausibly established, and even if it appears that we can plausibly explain a position in terms of vested social interests, we can never simply reduce the knowledge in question to social factors. While there are instances where social context appears to explain not simply an idea's success in society but also its origin and positive content, there are other instances where ideas appear to have anticipated and subsequently to have given rise to specific social contexts.

Given our initial assumption that thought and social structures exist in dialectical relation, we must also assume that there is no foolproof way of distinguishing the former from the latter. We can only offer our best guess as to how to interpret the relation in individual cases. Thus although we cannot prove that certain ideas are nothing but reflections of their social locations, we can ask their advocates to demonstrate that they are not, or at least suggest that they consider this possibility. If, for example, we can show that both the harsh denunciation and staunch defense of capitalism serve demonstrable social interests within a contemporary class conflict, this ought at least to move those who have used Scripture to make cases either for or against capitalism to examine their exegesis. One suspects that they might find that their use of Scripture has been forced or selective or both. This kind of critical self-examination is especially important for us Christians in our constant struggle to try to distinguish between the voice of God and our own will to power.

Our discussion thus far has presupposed that we are not interested in applying the sociology of knowledge to the biblical texts themselves, but only to our interpretation of these texts. But not everyone is willing to show such deference to Scripture and to exempt the biblical texts from the hermeneutic of suspicion. An increasing number of contemporary scholars have been asking questions like these. What if the very act of interpretation necessarily absorbs and transforms the meaning of these texts? What if it is simply not possible to speak of the "meaning of the text" apart from the circumstances and subjectivity of the interpreter himself or herself? While the sociology of knowledge perspective does not itself require us to answer these questions, it raises a number of troubling epistemological issues and points us in the direction of becoming increasingly suspicious of all texts and of all acts of interpretation.

But before we become too alarmed about the contemporary move to deconstruct all texts and all acts of interpretation, we need simply to recall that we do not as Christians claim any kind of epistemological privilege for ourselves, but only for Scripture itself. As Christians, in other words, we trust that God has been able to speak, indeed that he still speaks, *through* the flux of historical circumstance and sinful subjectivity *to* us, and not just mutely by way of creation or inarticulately by way of religious experience, but in *words;* specifically the words of Scripture. These are the words that are, as Paul wrote to Timothy (2 Tim 3:16), "God-breathed" and useful for teaching, rebuking, correcting and training in righteousness. As Christians standing in the stream of historic orthodoxy, we are committed to their binding authority. We take our cue in this connection from our Lord himself, who repeatedly insisted that the Scriptures *must* be fulfilled (Lk 24:44) and indeed that it would be easier for heaven and earth to disappear than for the least stroke of a pen to drop out of that which has been written in the Scriptures (Lk 16:17).

Unfortunately the contemporary intellectual context is such that the notion of *holy* Scripture is not much appreciated, for a kind of discursive autonomy or self-groundedness has ostensibly replaced appeals to traditional authority as the central measure of rationality. What we need to realize, however, is that there is no such thing as autonomous or "self-grounding" knowledge. All systems of interpretation and all claims to true knowledge are ultimately grounded outside of themselves and appeal, finally, to some norm or authority held to be above and beyond criticism. In science, this norm is presumably the nature of physical reality but is probably actually the validity of the scientific method itself. In the theologies of liberation, this norm is the experience of oppression. Indeed, even the most ostensibly hard-nosed, realistic and social-scientific theories rest upon a priori judgments as to the sorts of questions it is permissible to ask of them.

Some conclude from this that we must dispense with the notions of truth and error altogether, but even formulating such a proposition in sentences presupposes the possibility of meaningful (and therefore the possibility of *truthful)* communication. As Christians we are by no means alone in claiming a special epistemological status for the texts of Scripture, and we should not be embarrassed by this claim. Any act of criticism presupposes a fixed point from which to launch the critical project, and there is no more solid place to stand than on the Word of the living God.

This leads to a discussion of the theology of *revelation.* Without going into this theology very far, perhaps it will suffice here, at the conclusion of the chapter, to say that Christians have always affirmed *special* as well as general revelation. While this claim may be offensive to the non-Christian, there is no apologetic strategy that can lessen this offense. All attempts to do so have ended in either deism or pantheism. The Westminster Confession of Faith, an important Reformation confession, states, "The authority of Scripture . . . depends not upon the testimony of any man or church, but wholly upon God its author; and therefore it is to be received because it is the word of God." Christians believe that the Bible is the Word of God, in other words, because it is, in fact, the Word of God. And so we might conclude by saying that while our social situatedness may well distort or limit our understanding of Scripture, this does not prevent God from using Scripture to accomplish his purposes in the world, and indeed in us. His Word does not ever, as the prophet Isaiah declared, return to him empty.

5

Hermeneutics & the Postmodern Reaction Against "Truth"

Loren Wilkinson

*The god Hermes is the patron of thieves, merchants,
and travelers. . . . Hermes is cunning and occasionally violent:
a trickster, a robber. So it is not surprising that he is also the
patron of interpreters. . . . The rules of their art and its
philosophy are called "hermeneutics." This word, after
centuries of innocent use, turns out to have secret senses,
for it is thought by some to connote the most serious
philosophical enquiry, to be the means whereby they effect a
necessary subversion of the old metaphysics.*

FRANK KERMODE, *THE GENESIS OF SECRECY*

*By words the world was called
Out of the empty air,
With words was shaped and walled—
Line and circle and square,
Mud and emerald,—
Snatched from deceiving breath
By the articulate breath.*

EDWIN MUIR, "THE ANIMALS"

The entrance of your words gives light.

PSALM 119:130

In RECENT YEARS HERMENEUTICS has emerged from the cloister of biblical scholarship to become an important activity in the secular world of thought. Hermeneutics has cast its shadow across the whole range of scholarly activity: the humanities, the social sciences and even that bastion of (supposedly) pure fact, natural science.

What does this new centrality of hermeneutics mean for the Christian trying to live his or her life by Scripture? There is no quick answer—it lies at the end of a long and difficult path through the contours of twentieth-century thought. In the following pages we will walk that path in the confidence that God's word is a lamp and light for even this difficult way (Ps 119:105). And in the end we may know more about the light of the Word by which we walk.

In this broad new concern for interpretation, the fact that the discipline of hermeneutics has been honed by centuries of biblical scholarship has not gone unrecognized. Typical of the implicit secular appreciation of biblical hermeneutics is Frank Kermode's preface to *The Genesis of Secrecy,* which is an exploration of several problems in twentieth-century literary interpretation undertaken in the light of similar problems in biblical interpretation. Kermode acknowledges that

> the history of the rules and theory of interpretation—of hermeneutics as it used to be, before philosophy appropriated it—is closely linked with that of biblical exegesis; the exegetes drew up the rules or canons, refined them, distinguished between different kinds of hermeneutic activity, and expanded the whole subject to include such questions as what makes interpretation possible, how its process is affected by the lapse of time between the writing and the interpreting, what may be controlled by prescriptive rules of conduct, and what must be left to the divinatory genius of the interpreter.[1]

Kermode goes on to admit that secular scholarship has not "shown much interest in biblical criticism, except when it has seemed essential to research of the more antiquarian kinds."[2] And this, he says, is "unfortunate for several reasons. First, the scholarly quality and discipline of the best biblical study is high enough to be, in many ways, exemplary to us."[3]

At first the serious student of biblical hermeneutics is apt to feel a bit smug about this recognition. Is not the renaissance of hermeneutics a belated recognition of the worth of tools and techniques long guarded by the faithful?

But a careful look at the way hermeneutics is being applied is apt to cancel that smugness. Christians have long regarded biblical hermeneutics as the set of rules or the method by which the truth in a text can be made plain. Secular hermeneutics, on the other hand, increasingly seems to challenge the reality and objectivity of that very truth that hermeneutics once was supposed to illuminate.

Kermode's second reason to regret the long secular neglect of biblical hermeneutics illustrates a softening of the objectivity of truth. He points out the obvious fact that the practitioners of the Christian discipline of hermeneutics have been Christians. Their basis for interpretation has been (in the words of I. A. Richards), "doctrinal adhesion." Thus the truth of Scripture is not available to those who are not already to some degree initiated into the secret, the inner ring:

> In all the works of interpretation there are insiders and outsiders, the former having, or professing to have, immediate access to the mystery, the latter randomly scattered across space and time, and excluded from the elect who mistrust or despise their unauthorized divinizations, which may indeed, for all the delight they give, be without absolute value.[4]

Kermode goes on to illustrate his assertion by means of Jesus' troubling words in Mark 4:11-12: "To you has been given the secret of the kingdom of God, but for those outside, everything is in parables; so that they may indeed see but not perceive, and may indeed hear but not understand; lest they should turn again, and be forgiven."

Kermode is only one of many voices today using hermeneutics as an illustration that truth is neither as objective nor as methodologically accessible as many once thought it to be. His approach is part of a large-scale late-twentieth-century phenomenon which is called postmodernism. That label has been used very broadly, but it has the merit of identifying one significant common thread: an attempt to undo the damage associated with the "modern."

Bacon, Descartes, Newton: Three Sources of the Modern Mind

This is no place to give even the barest outlines of modernism, but the aspect of it that hermeneutic postmodernism is questioning is a particular notion of truth that came into focus in the seventeenth century. Three important architects of that model are Francis Bacon, René Descartes and Isaac Newton. In different ways they helped to shape an understanding of truth which has hypnotized Western thought for more than three centuries, and from which we are just now beginning to awake.

Francis Bacon was concerned with reestablishing human power over nature. He had good theological reasons for doing this, feeling that whereas we were created for dominion, we were all too much at the mercy of the nature we were meant to command. He placed the blame on the deductive method, an imperfect instrument of knowledge. Deduction (as evidenced in medieval scholasticism) was the result of pride which, like a spider, tried to catch truth in arid webs of speculation spun from its own innards. Bacon proposed a "New Organ" of knowledge, the inductive method, in which the humble mind would go from flower to flower of fact like the bee, gathering sweetness and light. To control nature, we first must learn from it. Bacon's picture of knowledge was to put away all initial ideas or premises and simply record facts. Taken together, the mass of discrete facts would yield truth, and truth would yield power.

Descartes (a younger contemporary of Bacon) was concerned to establish for all knowledge the kind of certainty he found in mathematics, and he began by doubting everything he could until he came to self-evident truth: "I think, therefore I am." This became the bedrock of his system, the axiom on which he proceeded to build his "discourse on method." For the purposes of understanding contemporary hermeneutics (which is largely a reaction *against* his thought) we will consider the significant features of the Cartesian method: (1) the world is a mechanical artifact: a structure of matter and motion which can be described by mechanical laws; (2) the individual mind sees, knows and manipulates the world from within the body; (3) the mind is "thinking substance," different from everything else (including the body) in that physical world of "extended substance." This picture suggests a lofty and lonely detachment from which the world may be known with perfect objectivity. (The Cartesian stance has been described as that of a ghost in the machine.) It is a sort of god's-eye view, a "view from nowhere."

Isaac Newton, toward the close of the seventeenth century, seemed to confirm Descartes's conviction of the machinelike nature of the material world by giving precise formulation to the laws of motion and gravitation. His picture of the stars and planets proceeding as if in a kind of clockwork captured the imagination of the next century and gave rise to the deist picture of a universe running so well on its own that God had no need to intervene. The godlike human mind was perfectly adequate to discern the laws of the universe and to use them for human benefit.

Whether Bacon, Descartes and Newton are really the architects of the modern mind or simply the best describers of something shaped by vaster cultural forces is not so important as the fact that they articulate three characteristics of modernity against which the contemporary "postmodern" fascination with hermeneutics is a kind of protest. From Bacon comes the emphasis on fragmentation, on breaking a thing down into parts before it can be known. From Descartes comes the ideal of detachment of the mind from what it knows. From Newton comes the compelling image of mechanism, of a universe which is the result of matter in motion according to precisely describable laws which the mind can discern. Implicit in all three, informing the whole of modernity, is the conviction that knowledge is power.

The contemporary preoccupation with hermeneutics in almost every discipline is a reaction against these early apologists for an unequivocal truth accessible through an infallible method. All that remains of those confident approaches from the beginning of the modern era is the concern for power. Kermode, for example, observes in the preface from which we quoted above that "the power to make interpretations is an indispensable instrument of survival in the world."[5]

Replacing Truth with Power

The most articulate contemporary defender of hermeneutics as a general approach to what was once called "knowing" is the philosopher (he is comfortable with being called a "neopragmatist") Richard Rorty. Toward the end of his 1979 *Philosophy and the Mirror of Nature* Rorty argues for the supremacy of interpretation in a chapter titled significantly "From Epistemology to Hermeneutics." He argues that epistemology (the study of what is true) is based on a false notion that there is such a thing as truth in nature, truth to which the representations in the mirror of our mind are more or less accurately conformed. Epistemology (says Rorty), through the whole modern era, has held out the false promise that through the proper procedure an appeal to truth could be made and all differences could (at least in theory) be resolved:

> The dominating notion of epistemology is that to be rational, to be fully human, to do what we ought, we need to be able to find agreement with

other human beings. To construct an epistemology is to find the maximum amount of common ground with others. The assumption that an epistemology can be constructed is the assumption that such common ground exists.[6] But, says Rorty, the search for common ground on which to resolve differences is futile, for there is no common ground—neither in a "correspondence" of our discourse with reality nor in a "coherence" of our discourse with itself. We would be better off to abandon entirely the effort to arrive at truth. Thus there should be no attempt to fill the gap left by the death of epistemology, the search for truth. What we must be content with, he says, is interpretation: hermeneutics. (This attitude is captured well in the title of a work by literary critic Stanley Fish: *How I Learned to Stop Worrying and Love Interpretation*.) Rorty's words make the difference between hermeneutics and epistemology clear:

> For hermeneutics, to be rational is to be willing to refrain from epistemology—from thinking that there is a special set of terms in which all contributions to the conversation should be put—and be willing to pick up the jargon of the interlocutor rather than translating it into one's own. For epistemology, to be rational is to find the proper set of terms into which all the contributions should be translated if agreement is to become possible. For epistemology, conversation is implicit inquiry. For hermeneutics, inquiry is routine conversation.[7]

In short, says Rorty, "this notion of interpretation suggests that coming to understand is more like getting acquainted with a person than like following a demonstration." In a somewhat later work Rorty expands his thought under the banner of neopragmatism and sees "language not as a *tertium quid* between Subject and Object, nor as a medium in which we try to form pictures of reality, but as part of the behaviour of human beings. On this view, the activity of uttering sentences is one of the things people do in order to cope with their environment."[8]

Rorty is probably the most lucid exponent of the principles underlying what we have called the postmodernist turn towards hermeneutics. But before we look at some of the many places in which it crops up in the culture, we need to consider several other sources. Together they help us understand the peculiar turn that hermeneutics has taken in contemporary thought.

Martin Heidegger

The first (in importance) is Martin Heidegger, whose massive and difficult

Being and Time is arguably the most influential work in twentieth-century philosophy. The work amounts to the first salvo in a lifelong "destruction of metaphysics" in which Heidegger tries to show that the whole philosophical tradition since Socrates has been sidetracked from the central task of human nature (which he calls *Dasein,* "being-there") into a search for ways of making definitive calculative judgments about things-in-being. That neglected human task is to create a space in which Being—mysterious, hidden—appears, comes to truth. (Thus he tries to restore a primal meaning of the Greek word for truth, *alētheia:* not correspondence or coherence but *a-lētheia,* "unhidden-ness" or "disclosure.")

In *Being and Time* there appears a brief but potent discussion of the nature of interpretation which exerts enormous influence on twentieth-century theology, first through Heidegger's colleague at Marburg, Rudolf Bultmann, and later through Heidegger's student, Hans-Georg Gadamer. Heidegger's discussion of hermeneutics (section 32 of *Being and Time*) is set in his introductory discussion of "the phenomenological method of investigation" (section 7). Heidegger's thought—indeed, the whole ascendancy of hermeneutics over epistemology—can be seen as one dimension of phenomenology. (Phenomenology is that concern with the analysis of lived experience which originated in Heidegger's teacher, Edmund Husserl.)

Heidegger defines phenomenology in such a way as to sidestep the characteristically modern way of knowledge summed up above in Bacon's inductivism, Descartes's detachment and Newton's mechanism. He suggests that phenomenon (from the Greek *phainō,* to show forth) can best be understood as "the showing itself in itself." And *logos,* from *legein,* can best be understood as "letting-be-seen." Phenomenology therefore means "to let that which shows itself be seen from itself in the very way it shows itself from itself."[9] The point of that outrageous definition is to establish the possibility of a way of knowing which does not "stand over" the thing known, but rather "lets it appear": does not impose a method but approaches what is to be known with enough humility to let it speak.

In Heidegger's later discussion of hermeneutics he continues to try to define a human *activity* of knowing which is at the same time not an imposition of what is already known. Heidegger says that every experience of meaning is centered ultimately not in the thing known, but in the knower. Here is his difficult (but unavoidable) way of putting it:

> In so far as understanding and interpretation make up the existential state of Being of the "there" [Heidegger is referring here to *Da-sein* there-being, his name for humanity, the only thing in Being which interrogates being], "meaning" must be conceived as the formal-existential framework of the disclosedness which belongs to understanding. Meaning is an *existentiale* [a term which Heidegger uses to mean a necessary element of *dasein's* existence] of Dasein, not a property attaching to entities, lying "behind" them, or floating somewhere as an "intermediate domain." Dasein only "has" meaning, so far as the disclosedness of Being-in-the-world can be "filled in" by the entities discoverable in that disclosedness. *Hence only Dasein can be meaningful or meaningless.* That is to say, its own Being, and the entities disclosed with its Being, can be appropriated in understanding, or can remain relegated to non-understanding.[10]

The notorious difficulty of Heidegger's language causes many thinkers in the Anglo-American analytical tradition to conclude that in passages like this he is saying nothing at all. But what many have taken him to be saying in this and other passages is that meaning is a property not of things themselves but of our way of knowing; at the same time it is not an imposition on entities (texts) but is rather the field or horizon in which the Being of things is disclosed—in a necessary dialogue with the knower.

Heidegger recognizes and welcomes the circularity of this picture of interpretation:

> What is decisive is not to get out of the circle but to come into it in the right way. This circle of understanding is not an orbit in which any random kind of knowledge may move; it is the expression of the existential *fore-structure* of Dasein itself. It is not to be reduced to the level of a vicious circle, or even of a circle which is merely tolerated. *In the circle is hidden a positive possibility of the most primordial kind of knowing* [emphasis mine].[11]

The notion that interpretation is inescapably circular is certainly nothing new to hermeneutics, but it has always been recognized as a kind of peripheral paradox. Heidegger, however, places that circularity at the center of interpretation—as he places interpretation at the center of knowing.

Hans-Georg Gadamer

This central circularity is taken up by Heidegger's student Hans-Georg Gad-

amer, whose work *Truth and Method* has been a major direct influence on
the new hermeneutics. Two elements of Gadamer's thought are central. The
first is a rejection of what he calls the "prejudice against prejudice."[12] Drawing
on the Heideggerian passages we have just considered, he affirms that "understanding inevitably involves some prejudice." That prejudice should not be
exorcised but named and welcomed as a basis for understanding:

> A person trying to understand a text is prepared for it to tell him some-
> thing. That is why a hermeneutically trained mind must be, from the start,
> sensitive to the text's quality of newness. But this kind of sensitivity in-
> volves neither "neutrality" in the matter of the object nor the extinction of
> one's self, but the conscious assimilation of one's own foremeanings and
> prejudices.[13]

Thus in Gadamer's view there is no such thing as an impersonal method which
one applies to a text to arrive at its meaning. Meaning emerges in relationship
to the interpreter, which means that one can no longer appeal only to the
author's intention as the arbiter of meaning. (Thus Gadamer conforms to
Rorty's rejection of epistemology as a means by which one can settle disagree-
ments by referring to an absolute standard—in this case the author's intention.)

"Not occasionally only, but always, the meaning of a text goes beyond its
author. That is why understanding is not merely reproductive, but always a
productive attitude as well. . . . Suffice it to say that one understands differently when one understands at all."[14] Thus Gadamer rejects all three of the
root characteristics of modernism outlined above: Cartesian detachment, Baconian fragmentation and Newtonian mechanism. The text is not an object to
be worked on by reducing it to discrete problems to be solved by applying the
proper laws; it is rather a sort of field in which meanings play and are disclosed. This leads to Gadamer's second major contribution to hermeneutic
thought: the idea of meaning as the "fusion of horizons."[15]

The reader comes to the text within the horizon of his own world. Likewise
the text itself has its horizon (which is not the horizon of the author). When
those two horizons merge or fuse, meaning occurs. Thus the meaning of a text
is not fixed by the author's intention (or anything else) but always emerges
in the conversation between text and reader. (Again, the similarity to Rorty's
rejection of epistemology in favor of interpretation is evident.)

Gadamer is aware that to cut meaning loose from the intention of the author opens the door to relativism and a complete indeterminacy of meaning. In defense against such relativism, he argues for the assimilation of tradition which links the interpreter and the author. That gap of time "is not a yawning abyss but is filled with the continuity of custom and tradition, in the light of which all that is handed down presents itself to us."[16]

Many have argued (especially E. D. Hirsch in *Validity in Interpretation*) that this appeal to tradition is an inadequate guarantee against relativism:

> For the concept of tradition with respect to a text is no more or less than the history of how a text has been interpreted. Every new interpretation, by its existence belongs to and alters the tradition. Consequently, tradition cannot really function as a stable, normative concept, since it is in fact a changing, descriptive concept. . . . Without a genuinely stable norm we cannot even in principle make a valid choice between two differing interpretations, and we are left with the consequence that a text means nothing in particular at all.[17]

The way Gadamer's ideas have since been used suggests that Hirsch is right: tradition is an inadequate guard against relativity. But before looking at the outworking of these ideas, we need to consider some other background.

Though the thought of Heidegger and Gadamer provides the largest philosophical component of the "new hermeneutic," the movement as it has emerged in popular culture draws heavily not only on Heidegger and Gadamer but on two nineteenth-century thinkers (Nietzsche and Marx), two recent French theorists (Jacques Derrida and Michel Foucault) and a murky movement of literary and culture criticism known as deconstruction. Their thought too must be surveyed before we can evaluate the Christian implications of this approach to hermeneutics.

Friedrich Nietzsche

In a troubling book called *Erring: A Postmodern A/theology,* Mark Taylor declares that "deconstruction is the 'hermeneutic' of the death of God." He makes the statement after a reflection on the significance of the proclamation by Nietzsche (whom he calls "one of the greatest prophets of postmodernism") that "God remains dead. And we have killed him." Taylor quotes as well the opening lines of W. B. Yeats's great poem "The Second Coming," in which Yeats identifies the sense in which God *has* "died" *from the viewpoint of the culture* in a sense that even believers must affirm:

> Turning and turning in the widening gyre
> The falcon cannot hear the falconer;
> Things fall apart; the centre cannot hold;
> Mere anarchy is loosed upon the world.

Christians are understandably uneasy about the phrase "the death of God." But we should not let the short-lived silliness of the death of God movement in the sixties obscure the significant point about our culture which Nietzsche was the first to make clearly. The civilization is no longer (in Yeats's phrase) "centered" on the eternal realities of God. It is thus cast adrift, wandering. There is nothing to undergird values so they become simply *my* values. Nietzsche alone in the optimistic European civilization of the late nineteenth century recognized the seriousness of the situation. A century later we are beginning to understand what he meant. For example, people talk of *choosing* their values, and courts struggle to resolve knotty issues like abortion and the nature of human personhood without any transcendent reference.

Nietzsche's solution to this grave situation was to recognize that the strong man must live boldly "beyond good and evil." This meant in effect that he had to give up the idea of any standard for action outside himself; he had nothing left besides the "Will to Power." Thus the *Übermensch* (superman) had no choice but to create his own values and live by them.

Nietzsche predicted that his word had come too early, and in fact it was not widely heard until our own time. Now it has been heard and has become a potent cultural force through a kind of alliance with certain themes in Marxism.

Karl Marx

A central idea of Marxism is that religions and philosophies—indeed most of human culture—are a "superstructure" built on the "substructure" of economic relationships. Such superstructures are in effect interpretations of reality, and according to Marx they are always controlled by those who have economic power. The famous Marxist dictum that religion is the opiate of the people reflects this analysis. As a master might keep his workers in virtual slavery by providing opium to allow a brief escape from misery, so, Marx said, a world of bliss after death was a useful fiction to keep workers from changing their present state. But Marx did not direct his criticism against religion only. He criticized *any* theoretical understanding that impeded action, maintaining that it is not as important to *understand* the world as it is to change it.

Later Marxism found this understanding of all interpretations as being in the control of a power elite to be a useful tool. It is based on the assumption that human relationships are essentially power relationships between oppressed and oppressor. Thus Marxist thought has stressed consciousness-raising, which enables people to identify their oppressor and then identify the stories, interpretations or pictures of reality that perpetuate that oppression. In this view it is imperative for the oppressed to throw off both the oppressor and the accompanying superstructure of interpretations.

Deconstructionist Criticism

The movement known as deconstructionism first emerged (under that name) as a school within academic literary criticism, though it has since obtained a much wider influence. Literary criticism in general is a kind of secular hermeneutics of nonbiblical texts, and it has been on uncertain ground for at least as long as it has been an academic discipline. One twentieth-century attempt to place it on firmer ground was called structuralism. Structuralism was rooted in anthropology and psychology and argued that literary works functioned as structures of words which provide meaning for people facing meaninglessness—much as totemic systems or clan organization (for example) could provide ways of structuring a primitive people's otherwise chaotic universe.

Whereas structuralism argued that there is a kind of single meaning in these structures, poststructuralism or deconstructionist criticism makes the case that any text has a multiplicity (indeed, an infinity) of meanings, any one of which undoes or contradicts the other. Jonathan Culler clarifies the distinction:

> In simplest terms, structuralists take linguistics as a model and attempt to develop "grammars"—systematic inventories of elements and their possibilities of combination—that would account for the form and meaning of literary works; post-structuralists investigate the way in which the project is subverted by the workings of the texts themselves. Structuralists are convinced that systematic knowledge is possible; post-structuralists claim to know only the impossibility of this knowledge.[18]

Jacques Derrida

The best-known defender of deconstructionist criticism is the French philosopher Jacques Derrida. His system is difficult to summarize—and to understand—because central to it is the conviction that since (in Yeats's phrase) "the centre cannot hold," every assertion, every meaning, can and should be undercut, challenged, "deconstructed." Without some center of transcendent meaning (in Derrida's words), "everything becomes discourse . . . that is to say, a system in which the central signified, the original or transcendental signified, is never absolutely present. . . . The absence of the transcendental signified extends the domain and the play of signification infinitely."[19]

We are left only with conversation, discourse, the play of language. That concept of "play" (important also to Gadamer) is another key idea in Derrida. He uses it to undercut the seriousness implicit in the idea of an absolute or transcendent center. There is only a "field" of significations which elude (or subvert) any attempt to pin them down: "One could call *play* the absence of the transcendental signified as limitlessness of play, that is to say as the destruction of onto-theology and the metaphysics of presence."[20]

There is thus a frustrating whimsicality to much of Derrida's writings, in which, consistent with his own theory (for example), he asserts in one column what he challenges in a column parallel to it. He is seeking to communicate the idea that no communication, including his own, has any one single significance.[21]

Michel Foucault

An attitude of meaning-eluding playfulness may characterize Derrida, but the other major theorist of deconstructionism, Michel Foucault, is much more serious. To the rejection of "onto-theology" or "the metaphysics of presence" Foucault weds the essentially Marxist idea that *every interpretation is put forward by those in power.* According to these thinkers, knowledge (since there is no "presence" to which it refers) is *only* interpretation. Foucault ranges across Western culture with an analysis based on the idea that knowledge is always the result of the use of power, always the construction of those who are the victors in some kind of struggle. "Truth," he says, "is linked in a circular relation with systems of power which produce and sustain it, and to effects of power which it induces and which extend it. A regime of truth."[22]

Foucault examines schools, prisons, asylums, businesses, families—most of the institutions that organize modern life. His conclusion is that concepts like "criminal," "perverted" and "insane," though they apparently describe an objective reality, are always imposed from the outside, are always ways of waging power. He notes the elaborate way in which accounting procedures arose in business as ways of providing an apparently objective and indisputable story to justify a company's policies and procedures. About the same time that formal accounting procedures came into business, numerical grading procedures spread throughout education. All such measures—from labels like "certifiably insane" to percentage grades on an essay test—are, according to Foucault, interpretations for the purpose of gaining power, and they necessarily subvert and do violence to the interpretation of another.

With regard to social and political institutions, Foucault inverts Clausewitz's famous statement that "war is the continuation of politics by other means" to "politics is the continuation of war by other means."[23] War, the violent exercise of power, is the basic human relationship, and other social institutions—political, familial, even charitable—are disguised ways of exercising power. They all do violence by imposing a certain understanding of "truth" on the centerless flux of experience. In Foucault's words:

> One is driven to ask this basic question: isn't power simply a form of warlike domination? Shouldn't one therefore conceive all problems of power in terms of relations of war? Isn't power a sort of generalised war which assumes at particular moments the forms of peace and the State? Peace would then be a form of war, and the State a means of waging it.[24]

The Old Testament: A Christian "Deconstruction"

We may seem to have moved a long way from biblical hermeneutics, but in fact we have come full circle. We began by noting Frank Kermode's appreciation for the tradition of biblical interpretation—and his acknowledgment that it has traditionally been carried out within the church. But Kermode understands that ecclesiastical horizon of biblical interpretation to always be a form of control and authority. In Foucault's terms, biblical interpretation, like all interpretation and *all knowledge,* takes place within a structure in which knowledge is power. Kermode proceeds to point out a specific case by quoting John Hollander, who speaks of "this new form of interpretation whereby . . . a previously non-existent book, called the Old Testament, is created out of an old one, the Torah." As a result, says Kermode,

> a whole literature, produced over many centuries and forming the basis of a highly developed religion and culture is now said to have value only as it complies with the fore-understanding of later interpreters. The interest

of these latecomers is solely in certain arcane figurations to which all who had supposed themselves the proper interpreters of that literature were deaf and blind.[25]

Thus in the eyes of some the very formation of the canon into old and new testaments reflects the exercise of power which Foucalt describes. To sense that "violence," we need look no further than the phrase "Judeo-Christian tradition" and the distaste most Jewish scholars feel for it. As Michael Lodahl suggests, the phrase "Judeo-Christian tradition" (not a phrase used by Jewish scholars who take their faith seriously) masks an "ideological violence . . . perpetuated for two millennia: beneath the appearance of congenial assimilation lurks presumptuous displacement."[26]

Nor is an argument that interpretation yields not truth but a kind of violence limited to biblical criticism and (via Foucalt) theoretical social science, as we will see in the following discussion.

Some Deconstructive Interpretations

1. In theologies of "liberation." Deconstructionist attitudes are implicit in various theologies of liberation. Liberation theology originated in the self-conscious attempt by Latin American Christians to apply the gospel to their situation of poverty. The problem of the sources of poverty is particularly vivid in Latin America, for it is a culturally Christian region in which there are extreme differences between the rich and the poor. Yet both rich and poor affirm allegiance to the same Bible. José Míguez Bonino (in an important early book called *Doing Theology in a Revolutionary Situation*) recounts the story of a Puerto Rican theologian who was in prison for a political demonstration. He was trying to show how his action was anchored in his Christian faith when he was cut short by a fellow prisoner: "Listen, your faith does not mean a thing, because you can justify your political course of action and the man who put you in prison can do the same, appealing to the same truth."[27]

From this sort of dilemma has emerged a school of interpretation in which "reality is the main text"—that is, one's political and economic situation is recognized as the necessary horizon for understanding Scripture. Says Míguez Bonino, "Every interpretation of the texts which is offered to us (whether as exegesis or as systematic or as ethical interpretation) must be investigated in relation to the praxis from which it comes."[28]

Míguez Bonino identifies Marx and Freud as "the two modern masters of 'suspecting.' " He is referring to the Marxist idea that all metaphysical and religious systems are a superstructure built on the more fundamental substructure of economic relationship. He continues:

> We cannot receive the theological interpretation coming from the rich world without suspecting it, and, therefore, asking what kind of praxis it supports, reflects, or legitimizes. Why is it, for instance, that the obvious political motifs and undertones in the life of Jesus have remained so hidden to liberal interpreters until very recently?[29]

Míguez Bonino goes on to warn against the complete relativization of the biblical message and makes a strong case for the need to use all the tools of objective interpretation: "historical, literary, traditio-historical, linguistic."

But the recognition that the foundation of interpretation is praxis, not theory, opens the door through which a crowd of less circumspect theologians of liberation have come. They have in common the need to raise the consciousness of the interpreter before a proper interpretation can be arrived at, and the consciousness which is to be raised is one's consciousness of oppression. Implicitly the Bible has become a resource for liberation—but liberation from forces which are defined (usually) in extrabiblical terms. Peter Berger points out the fatal flaw in the "conscientization" approach:

> A good way to begin a critique of the situation is to concretize it sociologically. *Whose* consciousness is supposed to be raised, and *who* is doing the raising? . . . "Consciousness-raising" is a project of higher-class individuals directed at a lower-class population. It is the latter, *not* the former whose consciousness is to be raised.[30]

Berger is criticizing the fact that Foucault (following Marx) said is inevitable and unavoidable: the "truths" that our interpretations yield are always truths that benefit someone but discomfort others. Truth is not understood as a penetration to some essence or ontological presence but as a means to power, a way of coping.

Latin American liberation theology—for all the danger of its root premise—is addressed to genuine and undeniable oppression. The weakness of the hermeneutic on which it is based is more obvious when it becomes a sort of blanket invitation for all people to question the ways in which they are oppressed. Thus women's liberation has adopted, for the most part, the approach (and even the vocabulary) of Latin American liberation theologians. Elisabeth Schüssler Fiorenza, for example, in *Bread, Not Stones,* argues that women must begin by naming their situation of oppression and then turning to the Bible to find the means to liberation. There is no question that women have been—and are—oppressed. But the nature of that oppression is often not so clear (and perhaps not helpfully understood under labels like "oppression"). In any case the oppression is more subjectively defined, and consciousness of it even more dependent on a political agenda. Such arbitrariness in defining oppression becomes even more obvious in gay theology, where heterosexuality is defined as an oppressive system from which homosexuals must be liberated.

2. In "politically correct" language. The movement reaches its logical conclusion in the call for "politically correct" language. In recent years there has been a growing awareness that the labels we use to describe groups of people are often not chosen by the people themselves. Words like *Negro, colored* and even *black* are all more or less veiled ways of saying "nigger" because (it is argued) the labels have been applied by the people in power—who are not the people being labeled. Thus the current politically accepted phrase is "people of color." Likewise Christians, Jews, Muslims and others are delivered from the possible bias of those words and grouped under "people of faith." The stigma associated with crippled, handicapped or retarded is avoided by the phrase *differently abled;* the male shadow over "women" is eliminated with "womyn"—and so forth. In recent decades we have seen large segments of the world's nations pass rapidly, in global discourse, through labels like *former colony, poor, underdeveloped, developing, less developed, Third World* and *Two-Thirds World.*

What is being sought in all these labels is a name that does not imply an interpretation. Interpretations are imposed by people in privileged position and (so it is argued) always distort. They imply that the thing labeled must be seen according to a picture of reality that is imposed as truth. But (and here we go back to the deconstructionist rejection of "metaphysics of presence") there is no "truth" as such, only an endlessly shifting series of interpretations by which people assert their power over their environment and each other.

3. In resistance against a "core curriculum." One of the battlefields on which this war against "epistemological privilege" has been fought is the idea of a core curriculum that every person ought to know if she (or he)[31] is to be regarded as educated. For several centuries there was only peripheral debate about what that curriculum ought to be. Everyone agreed it should draw on classics from Greek and Latin antiquity, the Bible, and the philosophic, literary and scientific works of Western culture. But recently it has been argued that there is nothing ontologically central about Western culture. It is, after all, largely the creation of white, empowered males and thus is simply one more interpretation imposed by a power structure. Why then should the works of Homer, Dante and Shakespeare be preferred over Nigerian folk tales, Hindu epic and lesbian poetry?

4. In the interpretation of the past. Not surprisingly, history—as it has traditionally been thought of—has come in for a great deal of criticism in this hermeneutically obsessed movement. Of course questioning the objectivity of history is nothing new. Though some may still regard history as nothing more than the accumulation of uninterpreted fact, historians have always recognized that it is a selective telling of a story. But they always (consciously or not) have assumed some transcendent process or direction in the events they are describing, and thus a shape of truth (however hard to achieve) to the story. The movement I have been describing has radicalized the notion that there is one truth or history that coordinates all the rest. It assumes that history is told by the winners and that it is therefore necessary for every group to create its own history. The goal in some cases is not that the redone history is more "true," but that it is more useful.

The likely endpoint of this is, not surprisingly, a skepticism about making sense out of human affairs at all. A description of the crisis in museum management makes the point clear. Under the heading "Deconstructing Expertise" a popular magazine explains the new problem that curators of a local museum have in knowing how to present their exhibits:

What does the label really say about the object? Why? And in whose voice?

These are questions curators . . . are posing as they adjust their exhibition practices to accommodate poststructural critical theories (like deconstruction) which refute the authority of the text. What text? Any text, including the researched labels and explanatory panels that have long been standard tools of museum exhibition.

Deconstruction theory says that because language is a shifting cloud of elusive meanings and ambiguous codes—and charged with cultural bias—it is impossible to establish with it any absolute or unilateral theme or story. Everything is flux and fragmentation. In a similarly disruptive fashion, deconstruction is applied to ways in which museums use and interpret material culture. "The postmodernist concept is one of fragments," [the curator] explains. "There's no truth, no one right answer."

5. *In the history of science.* The emerging picture is of no place to stand. Instead of certainty we find a "shifting cloud of elusive meanings and ambiguous codes." For most of the modern era science has been regarded as a source of reliable, objective meanings. But that too has been challenged in recent decades. The most influential work in this regard has been Thomas Kuhn's *Structure of Scientific Revolutions*.[32] Kuhn points out that histories of science have long given the impression that science has proceeded as a steady, continuous unfolding of truth. We know more than our predecessors, and our knowledge will necessarily be the foundation on which future science will be built. The actual progress of science, Kuhn argues, is very different. It proceeds normally within a certain hermeneutic or interpretive framework, in which key ideas provide a kind of paradigm (such as the earth at the center of the planets) within which science is carried out. But, says Kuhn, difficulties and anomalies develop in these interpretive paradigms so that eventually they have to be discarded entirely and replaced. To move from an earth-centered to a sun-centered planetary system was not a gradual development but a rejection of one model for another.

According to Kuhn such revolutions are the rule in science, not the exception. The reason we think otherwise is that the science textbooks (and the minimal history that they include) are written by the winners in scientific arguments. He points out that the people who challenge the old paradigms are almost invariably younger scientists who do not have tenure, books and reputations to defend. Knowledge is thus a matter of "paradigm shifts" (the ubiquitous postmodern term has its origin in this work by Kuhn) rather than gradual progression toward truth.

Kuhn's ideas have been enormously influential in the social sciences (not so much in the physical sciences which Kuhn is purporting to explain; this is a significant fact to which we will return). His analysis has been taken to prove that science itself is just one more subjective construction enabling us to make sense of an infinitely unknowable flux.

Richard Rorty (with whom we began this long journey through postmodernist thought) makes clear that he does not consider science to be a specially privileged form of knowledge, although he acknowledges that modernism, in its positivist form, was guilty of that mistake: "Positivism preserved a God in its notion of Science (and in its notion of 'scientific philosophy'), the notion of a portion of culture where we touched something not ourselves, where we found Truth naked, relative to no description."[33] Rorty prefers instead a kind of neopragmatism which "does not erect Science as an idol to fill the place once held by God. It views science as one genre of literature—or, put the other way round, literature and the arts as inquiries, on the same footing as scientific inquiries."[34]

In other words (as Rorty puts it elsewhere), "modern science does not enable us to cope because it corresponds [to the way things really are], it just plain enables us to cope." All the disciplines are seen on an equal footing, all based on interpretations of reality which help us to exercise power or, in Rorty's gentler language, to "cope." But we must, say all these postmodern thinkers, give up the modern idea that some method exists which gives us a god's-eye absolute view of truth. For we have neither that access to a divine perspective, nor is there any truth to which our various descriptions and interpretations correspond.

> Physics is a way of trying to cope with various bits of the universe; ethics is a matter of trying to cope with other bits. Mathematics helps physics do its job; literature and the arts help ethics do its. Some of these inquiries come up with propositions, some with narratives, some with paintings. The questions of what propositions to assert, which pictures to look at, what narratives to listen to and comment on and retell are all questions about what will help us get what we want.[35]

Thus we come to the end of this long survey of the sources and impact of the postmodernist turn toward "hermeneutics" in preference to "epistemology." But the most difficult task still lies before us: to interpret this changed attitude towards interpretation itself. What does it mean to us as Christians, committed to a God who has revealed himself in words and texts "at many times and in various ways," but especially "in these last days . . . by his Son, whom he appointed heir of all things, and through whom he made the universe"?

Postmodern Hermeneutics and Christian Faith

If we had to sum up the main thrust of the postmodern preference regarding interpretation, it would be something like this:

1. The modern project has erred (indeed the whole philosophical tradition since Plato has erred) by searching for absolute, objective knowledge that is accessible through a precisely definable method.

2. We need to recognize that understanding is tentative, personal, subjective and ad hoc. We do not have a god's-eye view of anything, so we cannot speak as though there were some ontological presence which our descriptions can mirror. What we have called knowledge is rather a shifting field of interpretations, necessarily competing with and undercutting each other. Knowledge is a way of coping, a kind of conversation; nothing more.

This absolute questioning approach has affected almost all intellectual disciplines, including the philosophy (though not the actual practice) of science. Should we let it affect our understanding and interpretation of Scripture?

It is helpful at this point to recall where we started: with a recognition that this movement is a peculiarly *postmodern* phenomenon. It seeks to move away from the excesses and dangers of the characteristically modern approach to understanding. We used Baconian fragmentation, Cartesian detachment and Newtonian mechanism as a way of characterizing key aspects of that modern approach to things. Have these modern attitudes toward knowledge skewed our interpretation of Scripture in any significant ways?

They clearly *have* been present in biblical hermeneutics, as they have been present in most of modern thought. A casual survey of the theses written on biblical topics by evangelical graduate students reflects the presence of all three modern attitudes. They are likely to be inductive, choosing a very small aspect of language, such as a particular word or phrase, for close investigation. Thus they exemplify Baconian fragmentation, the "divide and conquer" attitude of the modern mind.

Likewise serious study of Scripture is concerned with mastering a text in all its connections, as though it were an object or a system to be explained by various grammatical and syntactical laws. We are prone to treat the text as though it were a mechanical system of discrete parts whose meaning can be arrived at by the precise application of a method. The text is something to be worked: taken apart, analyzed, put back together according to various laws. Thus in our scholarship we often exemplify the mechanization of the modern mind.

Finally, we are likely to follow common scholarly practice in excluding reference to our selves, our passions and our prejudices in our exegetical and hermeneutic investigations. Associating objectivity with truth, we are likely to describe our findings in the passive voice, excluding any reference to personal belief or conviction. We even avoid using the pronoun *I*. Thus we exemplify the detachment characteristic of the modern attitude.

Of course this is an exaggeration. But certainly the tendencies described here will be recognized by anyone who has taken a course in exegesis or hermeneutics within the last half of this century at a school committed to the authority of the Bible. We seem to have concluded that we can best show our respect for the Word by subjecting it to the techniques of analysis perfected by the modern mind.

Roger Lundin puts very well the paradox of this approach. He quotes two writers, both of whom are seeking truth to live by. The first is Augustine in the *Confessions:* passionate, committed, anguished. He opens the Bible at random and finds the word from God which leads to his conversion. The second is Descartes: detached, calm, dispassionate, he sets forth the foundation of his method in his *Meditations on First Philosophy.* Says Lundin, "We live as Augustine and dream we're Descartes."

> As heirs of Cartesianism, we find that though our experience seems to indicate that we read as Augustine reads—as people who seek the truth, who are profoundly interested in that truth, and who belong to communities whose traditions mediate our understanding of what we read—we dream in our theory that we act like Descartes—that our reading of the Bible, of a novel, or the actions of an individual or group can be a totally disinterested, scientific affair.[36]

We probably have been too influenced in our hermeneutics by the modern ideals of detached truth, arrived at with methodological precision simply by moving from parts to whole. Knowledge is much more than this, so we need to hear these postmodern critics when they seek to bring the person, the knower, back into our understanding of understanding.

The postmodern reaction has gone too far in denying any "presence" behind a meaning, in dissolving meaning simply into a strategy for coping, and hence making all utterances equally valid. We have already alluded to the peculiar logical problem which makes such a conclusion unavoidable. If all interpretations are equally valid, then there is no way to misunderstand or misinterpret any text, including texts which argue (as do many of the ones we have been considering) that the author's intention is irrelevant.[37]

One of the most helpful discussions of this movement by a Christian thinker is an article by James Olthuis (a philosopher at the Institute for Christian Studies in Toronto) called "A Cold and Comfortless Hermeneutic or a Warm and Trembling Hermeneutic: A Conversation with John D. Caputo."[38] (Caputo is an American philosopher who is comfortable being called a "Derridean" deconstructionist while fearing the nihilism implicit in the movement.) Olthuis sees Caputo moving in the right direction in both appropriating and criticizing postmodern hermeneutics. I would like to draw on Olthuis's thought in moving toward a resolution of the hermeneutical problems raised by postmodernism.

Olthuis welcomes the challenge to epistemological comfort (the idea that *our* interpretation is the truth) which deconstruction represents:

> For Derrida there is no master story, or master name, no "metaphysics of presence," no Tradition. There are only stories, names and traditions. . . . Meaning scatters (disseminates) in the wind. Efforts to still the reality of flux by chanting a master name and constructing man-made islands of safety are inherently violent. Such totalizing moves have always historically left a wide swath of destruction and suffering, co-opting or dominating the "other".[39]

One need only reflect on the violence of religious wars, inquisitions and witch-hunts of every stripe to see the truth in this warning against any hermeneutics which is so certain that it turns truth into a weapon with which to defend epistemological privilege. Olthuis suggests that the Christian ought to applaud this prophetic dimension of the movement:

> For the Christian community which lives by love of God and neighbor the fundamental issues involved . . . are crucial and poignant. The reality of systematic violence, and of the marginalized, oppressed and voiceless in our day and throughout history is irrefutable.[40]

We do indeed need to recognize that the constructions of truth which we impose on reality have been the source of much pain and evil. Christians who have had the experience of being involved in a battle over some specific issue of biblical interpretation—be it eschatology, economics or the role of women in the church—know the rancor which can seep in, all the more because we are convinced that the book on whose interpretation we disagree is of ultimate authority. What good is an authoritative text, we say, without an authoritative interpretation? The question is valid enough. But most of our authoritative interpretations, say the deconstructionists, end up doing some sort of violence, either to other people or to other interpretations.

But is the only alternative to authoritative interpretation the "cold truth" of no truth at all? Caputo's reluctant conclusion is that "the saving message is that there is no saving message." That is cold comfort indeed, not acceptable to those who have experienced (despite, or by means of, human interpretations) the good news of God's saving message.

Olthuis points our way out of the dilemma by translating the discussion into theological terms. This he does by pointing out a complicated fact which I have, in my earlier summary, glossed over. In this discussion I have spoken as though Gadamer and Derrida are both representatives of a broadly postmodern criticism of "epistemology" (in Rorty's sense of epistemology as an infallible way of settling interpretive differences). That they are, but they also *disagree* significantly with each other.[41] Derrida accuses Gadamer of retreating from the full implications of his own thought by appealing to the "fusion of horizons" based on tradition. He calls him a "closet essentialist" and his philosophy a "crypto-foundationalism." Caputo (agreeing with Derrida) rejects Gadamer's appeal to tradition on the grounds that (as Olthuis puts it) " 'tradition' is for the most part the story of the winners."

In place of "tradition" Derrida proposes the centerless field of shifting and conflicting interpretations which we have encountered many times on this path. Once again, Olthuis describes eloquently the high moral ideal of deconstructionism:

> Deconstructionism attacks all concentrations of power—militarism, racism, sexism, academia, etc. [in this discussion we might want to add "theology"] and totalizing visions wherever they are found. All incarnations of the metaphysics of presence need to be deprivileged and uncovered as appearances, for it is in their name that minorities are excluded.[42]

As Hirsch has pointed out (see his comment in the discussion of Gadamer above), Gadamer places so much emphasis on the uniqueness of every encounter with the text that he effectively robs tradition of any real help it can give in settling interpretive differences. Derrida's radical deconstructionism would thus seem to be simply a more consistent application of Gadamer's idea that meaning always arises in the "play" between interpreter and text. From the viewpoint of traditional hermeneutics and epistemology, Gadamer and Derrida are quite close together. Nevertheless, the perceived difference between them can help us see the theological shape of the issue.

For us, the significant point in the "Gadamer-Derrida encounter" is that it highlights two apparently irreconcilable ideals. On the one hand, associated (rightly or not) with Gadamer, is the ideal of a "deep unitary truth" (Olthuis's phrase). On the other hand, associated with Derrida and the deconstructionists, is the ideal of manifold truth, "an unfolding of sense after sense in a process . . . of groundless play."

Olthuis suggests, with great insight, that two theological truths about creation and the human condition are concealed in this debate. We can generalize it to the whole debate between the modern confidence in knowing and the postmodern questioning of that confidence. Says Olthuis, the emphasis on an underlying source of truth and decidability "trades on the Christian affirmation that creation is called into being and sustained in being by the unitary Word/Spirit of God."[43] But to this unitary word of a transcendent God, revealed in Scripture and in creation, men and women respond diversely, incompletely and sinfully. Says Olthuis, "It is this brokenness and disruption in the responsibility-structures of creation which Gadamer . . . [and, I would add, the whole modern confidence in arriving at "truth"] tends to downplay and minimize."[44]

On the other hand, the deconstructionist approach—indeed, the whole postmodernist emphasis on the indeterminate flux of meaning—stresses "variety and difference. Derrida declares war on any system and its blessed possessors which declare that the truth is present in them. Better the . . . abyss of uncertainty than the totalitarian presence of meaning and its cauldron of oppression."[45]

There seems to be great wisdom here. The modern approach to understanding (on which confident evangelical hermeneutics is based) is itself rooted in a confidence in science which emerged in the seventeenth century. Bacon, Descartes and Newton are all exemplars of that confidence. What is not recognized often enough is that the whole modern scientific project is in turn rooted in a renewed confidence in the knowability of creation. Modern science—indeed, modernity itself—has Christian roots, as many thinkers have pointed out in recent years. Science has been seen as a kind of paradigmatic form of knowledge (indeed science *means* knowledge). That this knowledge is real, is in touch with something genuine and is not just an arbitrary shifting of paradigms (as Kuhn suggests) is evident in the rapid, irreversible growth of knowledge and the enormous impact of that knowledge when it is applied in what we call technology.

On the other hand, we have clearly overestimated the kind of knowledge which we possess and have used it for ill as much as for good. The history of our use of the knowledge of creation is full of what Olthuis (following Derrida and Caputo) refers to as fallenness, evil, rupture and distortion. Our response to the certainties (hidden though they may be) of God's word in creation and revelation is rooted in a God-given freedom and a kind of (dare we say it?) creativity which can only be understood by analogy with God's own. This freedom and creativity *is* God's gift. Yet one of its consequences is sin. Thus the confidence in meaning which underlies what Rorty calls epistemology is valid, rooted in God's self-declaring creation. On the other hand, the radical suspicion of all our attempts to fix God's meaning in our own systems and interpretation is valid too. It is the result of what we have made of our freedom, which is all too often sinfulness, distortion. Hear Olthuis again, commenting on a characteristically Derridean exegesis of *pharmikon* "which shows that it can either be a remedy or a poison." This ambiguity, says Olthuis, "need not demonstrate a basic undecidability or the indeterminacy of meaning. Rather on a depth level it may reflect the fundamental nature of created life before God: if we follow the lead of God's creative Word, a thing can be a remedy (i.e., blessing and shalom) for us, if not, this same thing can be poison (i.e., curse and disharmony).⁴⁶

Two great theological truths are illuminated and illustrated by this complicated discussion of hermeneutics. The first is the truth of creation: The earth is the Lord's, and in its very being, in its vastness, in its intricacy it is a testimony to both God's power and his faithfulness. *That* it is at all is a testimony to God's "word of power" by which it came to be. That it is both ordered and eloquent (for it does not remain silent in the face of our investigations) is evidence of God's faithfulness. Lying open to our investigations and our interpretations, it does not conform to them; rather, we must conform our interpretations to it, a fact which Francis Bacon saw very clearly. It is no surprise that modernity is rooted in the success of science, and science is rooted in the integrity of creation. Creation's ability to refute—or confirm—our interpretations of its order stand behind the whole modern era as a mute testimony to a reality which will not simply conform itself to our interpretations. The criticisms of the "metaphysics of presence" leveled by Rorty and others simply do not touch science, which proceeds in its inexhaustible dialogue with the given of creation as though it were real. Science reminds us steadily that truth is not simply a human projection onto Nothing. It is a response to Something.

The second truth is really, in theological terms, *two* truths, though they need first to be addressed together because deconstructionism does so. Then we must distinguish them carefully, for only in so doing lies the possibility of a fully biblical response to the whole broad movement of postmodernist hermeneutics which we have been addressing.

We are speaking of the fact of human freedom and creativity. Christians share with the deconstructionists, from Nietzsche to Derrida, an affirmation of that freedom. But we do not share with them the notion that human freedom is intrinsically violent. For them "to be" means "to be in competition," so that every interpretation necessarily disrupts and deconstructs another's. There is no truth, only an interpretive war of all against all.

We cannot, from a biblical perspective, speak of human freedom and creativity without speaking also of a second fact, that twisting or distortion of freedom which turns it into the construction of self-centered and self-seeking worlds. Put another way, the truth of human freedom becomes a perversion as soon as it is affirmed without an awareness of the larger truth of creation—and our responsibility to the Creator—in which it must always been exercised.

We must not diminish the fact of either the freedom or the creativity. Some lines by a great twentieth-century master of "subcreation," J. R. R. Tolkien, describe our situation well:

Although now long estranged
Man is not wholly lost nor wholly changed.
Dis-graced he may be, yet is not
And keeps the rags of lordship once he owned:
Man, Sub-creator, the refracted Light
through whom is splintered from a single White
to many hues, and endlessly combined
in living shapes that move from mind to mind.
Though all the crannies of the world we filled
with Elves and Goblins, though we dared to build
Gods and their houses out of dark and light,
and sowed the seed of dragons—'twas our right
(used or misused). That right has not decayed:
we make still by the law in which we're made.[47]

Here indeed is the deconstructionist idea that our self-made worlds are endlessly shifting and recombining, and that such creativity is part of our nature, our right for "we make still by the law in which we're made." But there is a crucial recognition in Tolkien's words which is missing from the postmodernist hermeneutic: that we exercise that right in a condition of estrangement and disgrace. Human creativity is only subcreation. For all its freedom, it is still a *creaturely* act, performed within the constraints of creation. One of those constraints is the existence of other people and their intentions. We cannot spin out our creations—and interpretations—in ignorance of those intentions. For our subcreative (and our interpretive) can be (again in Tolkien's phrase) "used or misused." The deconstructionists recognize our tendency to make our subcreated words occasion for breaking the worlds of others, but they then conclude in a sort of nihilistic despair that there is no "creation" to which our subcreations are subordinate.

A reflection on the natural sciences can tell us a great deal. I have already noted that natural scientists (as opposed to social scientists and those in the humanities) are not much affected with Kuhn's pronouncements on the ultimate irrelevance of their explanations, for they seem to sense that though the paradigms may indeed shift, they are in dialogue with a mysterious, self-disclosing reality which transcends them and will not simply be bent to their interpretations.

Here the profound analysis of Michael Polanyi provides the context in which relativizing discussions of science (such as Kuhn's and Rorty's) must be seen. Polanyi's work is of enormous importance because it accepts the centrality of the personal, subjective, creative and communal dimensions of knowing without in any way denying the "presence" of something there to be known. Polanyi recognizes that knowledge is interpretation. But he does not let go of the fact that it is interpretation *of* an undisclosed reality. In the preface to his great work *Personal Knowledge,* he makes clear his rejection of at least one of the foundations of the modern:

> I start by rejecting the ideal of scientific detachment. In the exact sciences, this false ideal is perhaps harmless, for it is in fact disregarded there by scientists. But we shall see that it exercises a destructive influence in biology, psychology and sociology, and falsifies our whole outlook far beyond the domain of science. I want to establish an alternative ideal of knowledge, quite generally.[48]

Rejecting the idea that detachment is a basis for knowledge, he aligns himself with postmodernism. But he does not take the fatal postmodernist step of denying the objective reality of creation, however subjectively it must be grasped. Polanyi affirms "the *personal participation* of the knower in all acts of understanding." He then continues:

> But this does not make our understanding *subjective*. Comprehension is neither an arbitrary act nor a passive experience, but a responsible act claiming universal validity. Such knowing is indeed *objective* in the sense of establishing contact with a hidden reality, a contact that is defined as the condition for anticipating an indeterminate range of yet unknown (and perhaps yet inconceivable) true implications. It seems reasonable to describe this fusion of the personal and the objective as Personal Knowledge.[49]

Like Gadamer, Polanyi recognizes that a "fusion" of the personal horizon with the thing known must take place if there is to be understanding. But Polanyi is much more confident, perhaps because he has a more robust sense of the *givenness* of creation—the objectivity, the reality within that other horizon.

The note which is present here is a kind of humility in the act of knowing or interpreting. This is a humility which does not evaporate into a rejection of the possibility of knowing anything at all. The interpretation must always be tentative, revisable. Later in *Personal Knowledge* Polanyi says,

> Why do we entrust the life and guidance of our thoughts to our conceptions [here Polanyi is using "conceptions" in a way synonymous with "interpretations"]? Because we believe that their manifest rationality is due to their being in contact with domains of reality, of which they have grasped one aspect. This is why the Pygmalion at work in us when we shape a conception is ever prepared to seek guidance from his own creation; and yet, in reliance on his own contact with reality, is ready to reshape his creation even while he accepts its guidance.[50]

The picture which emerges is of a knowledge which is tentative and personal but not necessarily less valid for its personal center. It probes with humility into a reality which will always transcend the knower. Polanyi recognizes the religious shape of such knowledge and notes its similarity to the stance of Christian thinkers like Augustine, who said that "unless you believe, you will not understand" and Anselm, who said "I believe in order to understand."

A Christian philosopher much influenced by Polanyi's thought is Jerry Gill. In a survey of epistemology called, significantly, "On Seeing Through a Glass

Darkly," Gill argues, following Polanyi, that all knowledge is "mediated knowledge." We never know directly. We know *from* a tacit and indwelt human center *toward* a reality which both reveals and conceals itself. We do not have a "god's-eye" understanding of anything. Yet our knowledge of any absolute (whether it be the structure of a molecule, the meaning of a text or God himself) can be sufficient, though always mediated, and always approached through our own faith and conviction. Gill suggests that though this is the shape of *all* knowledge, it should be particularly discernible by Christians because it is "an 'incarnational epistemology' wherein the mediator reveals the truth in a manner which is sufficient but not exhaustive. Jesus Christ is the glass through which we see reality, the medium in which we experience God."[51]

We are beginning to see a way of understanding which avoids the confident certainty of modern epistemology as well as the despairing "play" of deconstructionist hermeneutics. It recognizes that all understanding begins with faith. Far from blocking the way toward truth, faith opens the door to it. It is a way of understanding which affirms human freedom and creativity while acknowledging that such free creativity must be exercised within the limitations of the given of creation. This given meets us in the irreducible scandal of particularity, whether it be the particularity of a tree or a star, the words of another human, or the word of God. These eloquent particularities have their integrity outside us, yet they wait for the occasion of our understanding, our interpretation, to come to voice.

Many of the postmodern thinkers considered in this essay have drawn on the thought of Heidegger. Earlier in this essay we encountered his affirmation of the necessary circularity of interpretation, his recognition that meaning depends on *Dasein,* human nature. Later thinkers such as Gadamer, Rorty and Derrida have interpreted this to mean that there is nothing but subjective, free-floating interpretation, endless "coping" in a world bounded only by the interpretations of others. But this is overlooking the most important aspect of Heidegger's insight, which is remarkably close to a biblical one: all the subjectivity of our knowing is bounded and filled by the reality of "being" (we would say "creation"), always *other* than us, both withdrawing and giving. Our task is to create a space in which being can appear, to be a "shepherd of being." Heidegger pleads for a kind of reverence that he calls "releasement to things and openness to the mystery."[52] He argues for a "meditative" over against a "calculative" thought. By calculative thought it is clear that he means the kind of power-seeking manipulation against which the postmodernists are reacting:

> Calculative thinking computes. It computes ever new, ever more promising and at the same time more economical possibilities. Calculative thinking races from one prospect to the next. Calculative thinking never stops, never collects itself. Calculative thinking is not meditative thinking, not thinking which contemplates the meaning which reigns in everything that is.[53]

> The world now appears as an object open to the attacks of calculative thought, attacks that nothing is believed able any longer to resist. Nature becomes a gigantic gasoline station, an energy source for modern technology and industry.[54]

His words about calculative thought stand as a warning against any way of thinking which assumes that we can by applying the proper method simply get what we want, whether it be energy from a power plant, ore from a mine or truth from a text.

The alternative which Heidegger sketches, in a variety of ways in all his later work, is suggested by his early discussion of "truth" as *alētheia,* unconcealment. In this picture of truth *something* is unconcealed; it would remain hidden without the respectful approach to it of the meditative mind. Heidegger describes that respectful approach in a variety of ways and words. But basic to all of them is a kind of action that is at the same time a waiting: "Mortals speak insofar as they listen. They heed the bidding call of the stillness . . . even when they do not know that call. This speaking that listens and accepts is responding."[55]

A recurrent image in the picture Heidegger sketches of a kind of thought that "lets things appear" is a clearing or path in a forest. To think is to make a clearing or a path, an opening, around which the forest appears. This seems to be the picture by which he wants us to see the human activity of getting at the truth of something:

> In the midst of beings as a whole an open place occurs. There is a clearing, a lighting . . . the lighting center itself encircles all that is. . . . That which is can only be, as a being, if it stands within and stands out within what is lighted in this clearing. Only this clearing grants and guarantees to us humans a passage to those beings that we ourselves are not, and access to the being that we ourselves are.[56]

Heiddegger's language is itself elusive as he tries to describe an approach to things which neither overwhelms them with our method nor ignores the essential role which we play in leading out their truth. I suspect he is sketching a pattern which can teach us a great deal about interpretation. While recognizing the essential activity of the interpreter, he respects the meaning of the interpreted. Thus he neither acquiesces to the confident modern technicians of meaning-through-method nor does he deny (as so many of the postmodernists do) that there is real meaning to be found in our interpretations and not just the meaning of our subjectivity.

I have already suggested that this nonmanipulative approach to meaning is suggested in 1 Corinthians 13:12 (KJV), "Now we see through a glass, darkly." It is suggested again in 2 Corinthians 4:7 (NIV): "We have this treasure in jars of clay"—clay jars of human fallibility which nevertheless contain a treasure. We need not resort to Heidegger for authority to take a respectful approach to God's words and Word (though he may help us move in that direction).

We see such an approach outlined as well in the very well-known Psalm 19. It gives surprising confirmation to the path we have been trying to trace between modern calculative confidence and a kind of despair at no authoritative word or meaning at all. The point of the psalm does not lie in either of the familiar passages that are usually quoted without any reference to each other, but in the light that beginning and end cast on each other. They cast that light by means of the middle of the psalm, which is not nearly so well known. The key to the whole psalm lies in a paradox toward the beginning that has forced translators to disagree for centuries.

The beginning and end of this psalm are among the most frequently quoted passages in the psalter, if not the whole Bible: "The heavens declare the glory of God" (v. 1) and "may the words of my mouth and the meditation of my heart be pleasing in your sight, O LORD, my Rock and my Redeemer" (v. 14). These two passages seem to have little to do with each other and less to do with our tortured path through twentieth-century thought about interpretation and truth.

Both beginning and end of the psalm are about words and their meaning, which has been our concern throughout this study. A closer look at the opening verses shows an even deeper connection. But first it reveals a problem and a serious disagreement among translators. Here are the first four verses as they are translated in the New International Version:

The heavens declare the glory of God;
the skies proclaim the work of his hands.
Day after day they pour forth speech;
night after night they display knowledge.
There is no speech or language
where their voice is not heard.
Their voice goes out into all the earth,
their words to the ends of the world.

Not only, says the psalmist, does creation (as seen in the heavens) declare the glory of the Creator, but it does so in *speech;* it *declares* knowledge. Creation is a kind of text (an idea which has borne much fruit devotionally in the Middle Ages, and scientifically since the seventeenth century). But the plain sense of the words in verse 3 is so peculiar that many translators, including those of the NIV, shy away from it. But they do give it in a footnote: "They have no speech, there are no words; / no sound is heard from them."

It is easy to sympathize with the translators. How can any sense be made of a statement that the heavens have neither speech, language nor voice, when in the verses before they are said to declare, proclaim and pour forth speech? Better to give a reading which, though forced, makes some sense and put the apparently absurd literal reading in a footnote.

Other contemporary translators are not quite so timid. The Jerusalem Bible faces the contradiction squarely, rendering verse 3 as: "No utterance at all, no speech, / no sound that anyone can hear." Nor is the dilemma a new one. The King James Version translates, "There is no speech nor language, where their voice is not heard" (anticipating the more timid approach of the NIV). But the somewhat earlier translation in the Anglican prayer book takes the bolder, literal approach: "There is neither speech nor language; / their voice cannot be heard."

The easier rendering of verse 3 shows a desire to make of the text something that conforms to a modern sense of order. But wisdom suggests that we let the paradox stand without trying too quickly to resolve it. Reflection on the text as a whole resolves the apparent contradiction, and in so doing gives us a startling picture of the nature of the interpretation of any text, whether in the Word or the world.

Psalm 19 continues (after a vivid metaphorical picture of the sun) with a shift that is so abrupt that some commentators have suggested that two psalms are here patched together (another evidence of a modern penchant for clarity over richness). Verses 7-13 are an extended meditation on the Torah, God's revelation in words: "The law of the LORD is perfect, reviving the soul"; "the commands of the LORD are radiant, giving light to the eyes." So the psalmist proceeds, praising God's precepts, commands and ordinances. The psalmist expresses his delight in God's words: they are more precious than gold and sweeter than honey. And he recognizes that they are not simply to be contemplated, but rather that they are to be responded to, obeyed, so that they inform his own words and thoughts.

Then comes the well-known conclusion:

May the words of my mouth and the meditation of my heart
  be pleasing in your sight,
O LORD, my Rock and my Redeemer.

We are back at words, speech and wisdom, with which the psalm opened. But this time with a human center, and not without words or language. What is implied is that the mute meaning of the heavens is mute indeed unless it comes to utterance in the words of one who is properly open to them. And the only way that one can be open to them (can create the "clearing in being" which Heidegger calls for) is to delight in God's law, precepts and commands.

Only in the words of one who so delights and fears the revealed Word of God can the words of God become speech indeed.

A pattern that all our interpretations might take is here. Texts do indeed have their meanings and reflect their authors' intentions. But they cannot come to utterance until they become our speech, word, language (which is the exercise of the free gift of creativity from the Creator himself).

God's inarticulate words in creation can be understood only through being rooted in God's articulated words in revelation. More generally, meanings in texts are real; there is (contrary to Rorty et al.) a "metaphysics of presence." But they cannot be spoken without the proper human presence, a presence and approach shaped by a dwelling in God's revelation. As Proverbs 1:7 says, "The fear of the LORD is the beginning of knowledge," a statement that is perhaps the clearest answer both to the overconfident modern applications of method and to the despairing exercises of unbounded creative interpretation.

6

Toward a Biblical Spirituality

James M. Houston

T O THE GREEKS HERMES was the divine herald. He was believed to have invented language as a means of communication. It was in this context that the crowds at Lystra gave the apostle Paul a new name: "Paul, because he was the chief speaker, they called Hermes" (Acts 14:12).

Hermēneia means "communication." Philo calls Moses the "hermeneut" of God. A *hermēneutēs,* a communicator or interpreter, is required when someone speaks with tongues in the Corinthian church (1 Cor 14:27). Philip becomes an interpreter of the prophet Isaiah for the Ethiopian eunuch, someone from a different culture, language and religion. "With that very passage of Scripture . . . he told him the good news about Jesus" (Acts 8:35). So translation, interpretation and the bridging of worldviews and historical gaps are all expressive of hermeneutics.

But is there not something in the very act of reading itself that goes beyond this definition of hermeneutics? Public reading of Scripture, along with preaching and teaching, was a gift granted to Timothy (1 Tim 4:13). Jesus himself read publicly and interpreted in the synagogue in Nazareth (Lk 4:16). It seems to have been the practice of the early church to deal with the apostles' letters in the same way, to receive them and have them read publicly (see Col 4:16; 1 Thess 5:27). The intent of this chapter is to explore what reading means, to argue that the act of reading is more than translation, the interpretation of intent and the bridging of cultural gaps.

Do We Take the Primacy of the Word for Granted?

The "word," as something that can be orally transmitted, written down and then used to shape the life and behavior of a people, was central to the life of Israel. Hebrew was the most discursive form of ancient writing.[1] "Written with the finger of God" (Ex 31:18), the law was the command and personal will of Yahweh. "So Moses was instructed to write down all the words of the law" (Deut 27:3; see also Ex 34:27). Then the law was read by Moses to the people (Ex 24:7; 31:10-11), just as it was later by Joshua (Josh 8:8, 34) and Josiah (2 Kings 23:2).

Moreover, the biblical affirmation of Yahweh's work of creation is that it was shaped "by the word of his power." The divine action in creation is consistently referred to as *creatio per verbum* (Gen 1:3, 6, 9-11, 14, 20, 24, 26; Ps 33:8; 148:5; Jer 10:12; Prov 3:19; 8:27; Heb 11:3).[2]

The word by which the world was made is also the Word that was with God, and that is God (Jn 1:1). It is the Word that became flesh (Jn 1:14). The one reading the Bible belongs to a unique tradition of God's self-revelation given in his word, a tradition of listening to the communication of a personal God. Critical to this emphasis is the personalness of God. From this verbal foundation of biblical literature, law and history are seen as endeavors to embrace all human experience and its behavior as a record of God's dealings with humanity: past, present and future. It is no wonder that reading and hermeneutics have played such a central role in the shaping of biblical faith and its practice in the Christian life.

We cannot take for granted the universal centrality of religious language. In Eastern metaphysics, such as Buddhism and Taoism, the human soul is envisioned as ascending above the structures of language to enter into the deepening domains of silence. The highest, purest reach of the contemplative act is eternal silence, where language is left behind. Logic and linear conceptions of time are also left behind as past, present and future are simultaneously one. Language is perceived as an artificial construct that keeps them distinct. So the Eastern holy man withdraws from speech as well as from the temptations of worldly action. This profound distrust of language arises in the absence of a personal God. How different is the exegetical religious culture of Israel with its Hebrew Scriptures and the proclaimed faith of the gospel of the New Testament for Christians!

Since the rise of the secular spirit after the seventeenth century, there has also been a regression of language in the West. Many critics of mass culture today deplore the "retreat of the word." The broken sentences and staccato speech of a youth culture profoundly impacted by television reflect this. Dissonances in poetry and atonality in music, the manipulative use of words in advertising as well as the disposition toward the technical all led Lewis Mumford to charge that "the modern age has specialized in the debasement of language."[3] Marshall McLuhan has asserted that "the medium is the message." Herbert Marcuse has argued that the habitual repetition of standard catchwords and slogans has the effect of converting factual assertions into self-validating tautologies, true solely by virtue of the meanings ascribed to the terms used. George Orwell in the book *1984* expressed his conviction that the corruption of language leads to the corruption of thought, which leads in turn to the corruption of society. The secularism of the West leads to the death of communication. As Albert Camus put it in *The Rebel:*

> Every ambiguity, every misunderstanding, leads to death; clear language and simple words are the only salvation from death. The climax of every tragedy lies in the deafness of its heroes. . . . On the stage as in reality, the monologue precedes death, solely by the movement that sits in opposition to the oppressor, therefore pleads for life, undertakes to struggle against servitude, falsehood and terror, and affirms in a flash that these three afflictions are the cause of silence between man, that they obscure them from one another and prevent them from rediscovering themselves in the only value that can save them from nihilism—the long complicity of men at grips with their destiny.[4]

The systematic deterioration of language in times of crisis prevents dialogue when it is most needed and thereby contributes to the difficulty of obtaining the concerted action necessary to cope with the mounting complexities of our day.[5]

A new dark age in which humanity perishes by silence may be upon us.

Since Newton and Leibnitz developed calculus in the seventeenth century, large areas of knowledge have been submitted progressively to the modes and proceedings of mathematics, especially chemistry, molecular chemistry, biochemistry and other sciences. The so-called social sciences, following the fallacy of imitative form, are becoming increasingly caught up in the language of mathematics. The realm of the word is being compressed progressively, giving place to nonverbal forms of communication. This dooms us to an ever-increasing fragmentation of knowledge guarded by ever more specialized forms of technical communication, so that fewer and fewer people can understand one another.

Theology is not exempt. David Tracy, in his lucid advocacy of theological pluralism, calls for the differing exercise of theological communication just as the theological persona addresses the differing publics of the secular society, the academy and the church. These represent three differing mentalities on the principle of "being all things to all men."[6]

Scholarly researchers of the hermeneutical debate, with their theoretical disputations, seem to have little immediate application to the "act of Bible reading." Rather, that which is being applied to biblical hermeneutics is coming out of literary criticism with its secular spirit. Theory is to scholarship what power is to politics. The professionalization of abstraction proliferates in debates on hermeneutics today. The actual reading of Scripture is overlooked in all the scholarly talk. As the English literary critic Helen Gardner observed some years ago, it is the "scepter" rather than the "torah" that seems to reign in hermeneutics, with an unnecessary growth in professionalism.[7] Thus with a growing fragmentation or pluralism, increasing professionalization and the general degradation of language, we hardly know how to read any longer.

Reader Response Criticism

But the act of reading may be rescued from this threat by an approach to hermeneutics Anthony Thiselton calls "the two horizons."[8] The horizons, quite simply, are those of the reader and the writer. These horizons merge in reading, just as in a conversation each party discovers the context of the other. In his teaching (particularly the parables) Jesus entered into the world of his hearers so that they in turn might be able to enter into his realm of the kingdom of God. Thus a common understanding was made possible.

In the last two decades the philosophers of literary criticism have argued that a critic's reading of a work is itself an act of creative art. The phenomenology of "the act of reading" has led to postmodern hermeneutics, in which semiotics seems to replace hermeneutics in the complexity of investigating the reader's motives and understanding.[9] The act of reading is defined increasingly as a rhetorical act, indicating a radically more complex picture of what is involved in reading and of understanding the text. Some critics, in France especially, are thus seeking to go beyond hermeneutics.

Hermeneutics is quite simply the task of interpreting the text, whether one remains a "modern" or has moved into a "postmodern" school of thought. In an important article on the issue, Richard Palmer has distinguished between two trends in contemporary hermeneutics.[10] The first is indebted to the thinking of Heidegger and Gadamer, who see language as our way of being in the world, making it the inescapable medium of our interpretation of reality. It is the power of written utterance to evoke a world when read that makes it language. The reader thus appropriates what is read as his or her own in an act that involves self-understanding. Paul Ricouer argues that the act of appropriation is safeguarded from subjectivism by the prior processing of an "interpretive community," so that its meaning is not arbitrary to that believing community to which the interpreter has adhered. "The entire theory of hermeneutics consists in mediating this interpretation-appropriation by the series of interpretants which belong to the work of the text upon itself."[11]

There is a second wave of postmodern thinking that refuses to take the subjectivity of the human reader as its starting point. Thinking is focused on the conventions, institutions and linguistic structures per se that make textual interpretation possible—that is, an impersonal approach to reading. French postmodernists Jacques Derrida and Michel Foucault represent a position characterized by domination and scientific control through "knowledge."

If Kierkegaard is the father of the first wave of postmodern thinking, it is Nietzsche who opened the way for this second wave of critics.[12] Since God is dead for Nietzsche, truth is achieved neither by approximating to the divine mind nor in bringing our knowledge into harmony with God's will. "Reality" and "truth" are not absolutes. The whole enterprise of "knowing" is best called "interpretation" because it is "fabricated" or "fictitious." Since there is not first or primordial knowing, the residue at the bottom is merely illusion, motivated by the deeper will to power. Subjectivity is thus interpreted as merely warring and fragmented centers of power. There is no limit to the process and criticizing because there is no fixed point. It is as if looking through the window to admire the view, one only sees oneself ultimately in an endless process of looking through everything—window, view, anatomy of rocks and the whole geological gamut in all their nakedness and nothingness.

This negativity distinguishes and separates the "negative hermeneutics" of Derrida, Paul de Man and Edward Said from the ontological or reflective hermeneutics of Heidegger, Gadamer and Ricouer. The latter give a clear priority to the text over the interpreter. This is vital when it comes to interpreting Scriptures that purport to be the revelation of God himself. This approach does not see scriptures in the void of "the will to power" but places the act of reading in a personal context.

This act of reading has been construed differently in different historical periods and cultures, sensitivity to which sets conditions on interpretation. Such conditions include how one views the act of reading in prevailing discursive practices; the prevailing views of reality, or metaphysical worldviews of what truth is and of the way of knowing; the views and uses of what literature is and does for the reader; and the status given to the text as authoritative, judging, correcting, exhorting and the like. Such issues shape the view of the reader as to what interpretation is and what purpose it has in what it does, to affect or challenge the reader. It is facile to picture hermeneutics as merely commenting on a text; it is also engaged in the preconditions for understanding. Thus the role of the readers, their moral obligations to engage with the text, is central to valid literary criticism. But in postmodern negative hermeneutics the reader is displaced and decentralized to make "reader response" a meaningless activity.

Reading is not a mere act that experts can theorize about. It is also an art associated with social accomplishments through history. Reading has been (and still is) a social practice that can be studied through time as a history of interpretations. To these we now turn.

Reading for Exemplary Living in John's Gospel

A reader (Jewish, Christian or pagan) living toward the end of the first century A.D., when John the apostle was writing his Gospel, had only one rationale in being a reader. It was to acquire exposure to the classics, or indeed the New Testament, because such exposure produced exemplary human beings. Reading, argues A. J. Festugiere, was assumed "to produce exemplary beings, their raw humanity molded and filed away by a double discipline, at once ethical and aesthetic."[13] The purpose of books was to produce persons; any other purpose was vaguely ridiculous. The ability to speak and to act as one ought required emulating the best and shunning the worst.

This is what Henri-Irenee Marrou has called "the Civilization of the Paideia."[14] Later arose what the apostle Paul called the "saints," those who were "epistles of Christ, known and read by everybody" (2 Cor 3:2). Peter Brown has recognized the exemplar as characteristic of the culture of late antiquity: "the overwhelming tendency to find what is exemplary in persons rather than in more general entities. Despite a past littered with magnificent political experiments, a state of affairs never wielded the same exemplary power as did individual heroes and heroines."[15]

There was an intense bonding between the generations and the personal manner in which the culture of *paideia* was passed on. No student ever went to an impersonal institution like Cal Tech or the Sorbonne. A pupil always went to a person. In the New Testament context it was to Paul or Apollos, or indeed to Christ. Books also were to shape and develop persons; any other abstract motive was ridiculous. Classics were read to make people into classics. As Werner Jaeger observes, "Literature is paideia in so far as it contains the highest norms of human life, which have taken on their lasting and most impressive form." So Gregory of Nyssa interpreted the Bible as the Christian *paideia*.[16]

It is in this *classical* context that we read John's Gospel. John focuses on the characters depicted in his Gospel in order to attract readers to be like the positive exemplars of faith, to generate sympathy for inadequate responses and also to condemn negative readers through characters who rejected Jesus Christ. The juxtaposition of characters, helping to clarify the roles that appropriate hearing, knowing and obeying, plays a prominent role in John's Gospel.

This is believing in the apostle's intent. It is to integrate hearing with believing, trusting in the enunciator Jesus, so that in this Exemplar par excellence, the Savior of the world, human lives are radically transformed to live in Christ Jesus. This, in John's message, is what is implied in being a Bible reader. Thus biblical hermeneutics is seen as participatory living with the Speaker, as narrated by the "disciple whom Jesus loved." It is to believe or trust, remain or abide, not in theoretical or abstract truth but in the One who claimed "I am the truth," indeed, "the way and the life." John's Gospel is one of relationship, of the truth being the person of Jesus himself. In the classical sense of the exemplar, Jesus embodies what he is teaching as the Word who became flesh, the embodiment of his revelation of the truth of God.

In John more than in the other Gospels, Jesus is depicted as speaking with individual persons: Nathanael, Nicodemus, the woman at the well, the man born blind, Martha (before Lazarus is raised), Mary Magdalene (on the resurrection morning), doubting Thomas and Peter (at the resurrection). Each is a personal encounter with Jesus as the truth. Each is also a self-liberation, a freeing from destructive tensions and enthrallment with the self. Whatever self-reliance may mean, whether professional status (as for Nicodemus), traditional behavior (as for the woman at the well), personal inadequacy (as for the blind youth), going without evidence (as for Martha and Thomas) or behaving addictively (as for Peter), the truth in Christ both reveals and liberates.

In contrast, those who neither believe nor allow themselves to be liberated constitute "the Jews" in John's Gospel. If, as modern critical scholarship assumes, John's Gospel was written in its final form toward the end of the first century after the fall of Jerusalem and the destruction of the temple, then the theological problem faced by the Jews was how to cope with these disasters and reinterpret their "Jewishness" in the absence of both temple and promised land. The Zealots' political interpretation of fighting for power was set back by the fall of Masada (A.D. 73-74) and the failure of the Bar Kochba revolt (A.D. 132-35).

The rabbinic way, under the influence of Yohannan ben Zakkai at Yavneh, developed a form of Judaism that joined devotion to the Torah in the development of what became the Mishnah, the Talmud and other rabbinic writings. As Hengel pointed out, the strong process of cultural Hellenization abstracted the Torah as if it rivaled God himself, wholly rejecting that Jesus Christ is himself the Word of God.

Here the Christian faith parted radically from Judaism, and John's Gospel may be interpreted as a strong polemic at scriptural usage that is not Christ-centered. Whereas the Torah was given by Moses, "grace and truth came by Jesus Christ" (Jn 1:17). Indeed, Jesus is the One about whom Moses and the prophets wrote (Jn 1:45). It is rejection of this reality that makes "the Jews" the antagonists of Jesus in John's Gospel, whereas in the other Gospels it is the leaders, the scribes and Pharisees, only. In the depiction of opposition to his teaching (as in Jn 6:29, or later in John's passion narrative), "the fear of the Jews" runs prominently as the motif of opposition to Jesus.

In addressing this central issue of Bible reading, John uses various literary devices such as the court of law motif, witnesses arrayed on either side of the debate, the questioning as to what is truth, the reliability of witnesses. How does one interpret the Scriptures and live in light of them? In several of these personal encounters with Jesus, such debate freed the interrogator from his or her own prejudiced understanding. With "the Jews" it is a confrontation in which the whole discursive authority of Jesus' revelation of the truth is being rejected, as he himself is rejected.

The hermeneutical issue is where truth lies: in the scribal or oral tradition behind Torah, in traditionalism and the vested powers of inheritance? Is it not rather in "the Word made flesh," in "the voice from heaven"? Whatever witness John the Baptist and others may give to the gospel, the paramount witness is Jesus Christ himself, about whom the whole gospel revolves. Focusing on this, on being transformed by the personal presence of Christ in all the Scriptures, is what "exemplary reading" is all about. Beyond the text and page of Scripture, one is challenged and transformed by the person of Jesus Christ himself.

In the civilization of *paideia* in late antiquity, in which books existed to produce persons of integrity and appropriate deportment, John's Gospel would be read with deepest challenge. For what was read was expected to be expressed in a radical change of life, demeanor and behavior. Paulinus could respond to the teaching of his master by saying, *"Videbo corde, mente complectar pia, ubique praesentem mihi"*—"I shall behold by heart, by the mind I shall embrace the departed everywhere present to me."[17] What then should be the beholding of the Christian reader to the revelation of Christ in his Word?

The Use of Scripture Among the Desert Fathers

Within the complex world of ancient Egyptian culture, early Christianity spread from the Hellenized cities into the countryside during the fourth century A.D. The distinctive culture of the desert fathers also gave rise to a distinct hermeneutic. Although the majority of its Christians remained illiterate, living in a traditional oral culture, many of its leaders were highly literate, cultivating the new writing tradition of Christian apologetics.

Robin Lane Fox has suggested that "one of the fundamental contrasts between pagan culture and Christianity was the passage from an oral culture of myth and conjecture to one based firmly on written texts."[18] Yet this is only partially true, for the desert tradition of early Christianity is also a deeply oral culture. Entering into the sayings of the desert fathers is like entering into a conversation, to hear a word requested by the disciple. These words are stories, parables, sayings from daily life (probably in Coptic) which had a profound effect on the pedagogy of the desert monks. "Abba, speak a word to me" has the same effect as the Hebrew oral tradition of *dābār,* where the word connotes deed and action as well as thought and life, made possible only because it is God's word, given by his Spirit. This then gives personal salvation within our situation.

The "Abba" is recognized in these sayings as having a double skill. He is wise enough to discern and read hearts as well as to be an interpreter of Scripture. Both are based on personal experience. Then the word given is discerning indeed, setting the narrative of the disciple's encounter with the living Word, as a unity of discernment, application and renewed narrative. Out of this intensely personal, oral tradition, major collections of sayings by the Desert Fathers were formed and transcribed by the sixth century, only a small fraction of which have been translated. It presents a vast new realm for modern scholarship to collate and compare.

Scripture is interspersed within these sayings, not as the concentrated text we are habituated to in a writing culture, but diffused in the interplay of both oral and written traditions. As Benedicta Ward explains, "The language of the writings of the desert was so formed by the meditations of the scriptures that it is almost impossible to say when the quotation ends and the comments begin."[19] So the apparent paucity of scriptural texts is no evidence of the marginal use of the Bible, but rather the reverse. It is evidence of a thorough assimilation into the heart rather than a visual and mental use of the text.

Thus the words of the elders and the text of Scripture were interwoven into a living unity of obedience to both authorities. Scripture itself was recited each Sunday at the weekly public meeting or *synaxis,* while daily there was the twofold recitation of the psalms in private, following Anthony's injunction to "sing the psalms before sleep and after sleep, and take to heart the precepts of scripture."[20] Tensions arose over how such public and private reading or recitation was done, for legalistic practices of recitation were established in some communities. There was general recognition that it should be done in *humility,* to prevent a superficial nominalism of practice to develop. But with deep, humble openness to the Word, the result could be personal joy and social compassion as well as the cultivation of a discerning heart.

Meditation as rumination on the Word was widely recognized as an effective defense against temptations and demonic assaults within a life marked by silence and solitude. In this inner environment of the soul, psychological/spiritual depression *(accidie)* was a common ailment. Abba Moses compares the human mind to a millstone being turned by the water sluice:

> The mind, also through the trials of the present life, is driven about by the torrents of temptations, pouring in upon it from all sides, and cannot be free from the flow of thoughts. But . . . if . . . we constantly recur to meditation on the Holy Scriptures and raise our memory towards the recollection of spiritual things . . . spiritual thoughts are sure to rise from this, and cause the mind to dwell on those things on which we have been meditating.[21]

Scripture was capacious enough for the monks to relate deeply in their inner fears and wide enough to encompass all external temptations as well as higher than any soaring aspirations. Clearly Scripture was valued as having the most intimate as well as the most public bonding of their lives and communities.

In the desert words are magnified as sounds, while in village life words are circulated in mischievous and destructive ways. Monks had a profound suspicion of the misuse of words. A pure heart is needed to speak with integrity, without guile. Keeping silence helps to sort out the ambiguity of speech and seek obedience when the Word of God is recited. This creates a reticence to quote Scripture or speculate about it, for this is holy ground. This practical approach to Scripture marked the desert fathers, whether they interpreted in an exemplary, allegorical or ethical way. Originality of interpretation was not valued so much as consistency. For them a thousand years of exemplary teaching is far more significant than cleverness of scholarship in the transmission of faith. Moreover, intimacy with the text is related to intimacy with its characters, as exemplars of the faith. The biblical saints are, to such readers, daily companions, sharing intimacy with their own innermost feelings.

While Origen's speculative theology was extremely unpopular with the desert fathers, their own allegorical use of Scripture was common. But it was controlled always by ethical relevance and usage. Love of God was thus at the heart of desert hermeneutics. Their communities were schools of love: to learn to obey the commandments, to accept the high cost of love in asceticism, to overcome anger, to be nonjudgmental and to exercise compassion in sharing burdens and encouraging the fainthearted. The wisely discerning spirituality of the inner man of this tradition resulted in a remarkable tenderness of spirit in the midst of a harsh environment. It gave a quiet yet forceful sense of personal presence, to be *before* and *with* the other, under the Word of God.[22]

Lectio Divina and the Medieval Monastic Reader

Throughout church history the church's historical situations have significantly influenced the changing emphases of hermeneutics. The intense interest in eschatology during and after the second century gave way in turn to more focus upon Christology and then trinitarian doctrine in the fourth century. Origen led an interest in Christ's centrality in all the Scriptures. Origen had learned from his Hebrew teacher the tradition that "neither the beginning nor the end of all things can be understood by anyone, unless by the Lord Jesus Christ and by the Holy Spirit."[23] Beyond the literal interpretation of Scripture, for him, was thus the "spiritual" meaning, the gathering of God's Word into the heart. The spiritual, as distinct from the literal or grammatical historical meaning, was subdivided into three levels of meaning: (1) the allegorical or typological, which was basically a christological interpretation; (2) the moral or tropological, giving the moral correction needed for living before the Word; and (3) the anagogical or prophetic, concerning the fulfillment of Scripture.

As the monastic movement spread, rules of organization led to the written texts of Pachomius and later of Basil and Benedict. Larger communities, rather than small groups of disciples, engendered this. With the growth of the desert movements of asceticism and later of monasticism, "the written Word was seized on as a more accessible alternative to the charismatic authority of the holy man."[24]

Monastic life became one of *lectio,* reading the Scriptures and other books of devotion from two to five hours daily. This *lectio* was further defined as *divina,* "divine reading," for three reasons. Firstly, it was the text of Holy Scripture, the Word of God, that was being read. Secondly, it was so by virtue of the manner in which it was read, in prayerfulness and the slow rumination of life. Thirdly, its purpose was spiritual growth and transformation of life. In this way Bible reading was indispensable for spiritual growth.[25] *Lectio divina* has been variously translated as "holy reading," "prayerful reading," "meditative reading" and even "spiritual reading." It was exercised by the monks bodily, with the murmuring of the lips, with the meditation of the heart, with the memorization of the mind, throughout their lifetime in the conversion of the whole life before God.

Lectio divina reached its apogee in the twelfth century in the Cistercian and Carthusian forms of monasticism. Instead of teaching a lesson or studying the Scriptures critically, it taught prayer and involved the whole person in the service of God's Word. It created a mentality that disposed the reader to think easily and reflectively on God, in a calm spirit, in response and trust. Thus to learn something by heart and so expose the whole of the inner life, made it possible to represent actively what one had read or heard and to interiorize it so that the reader was freed from what today might be called its personal emotional addictions.

The psalms were focused on as summarizing the Bible itself. The Gospels, too, were often learned by heart. In his letter on the contemplative life, *The Ladder of Monks,* the Carthusian Guigo II gives us a clear expression of the fruits of *lectio divina* from the Middle Ages:

> Reading is the careful study of the Scriptures, concentration of one's powers on it. Meditation is the busy application of the mind to seek with the help of one's own reason for knowledge of hidden truth. Prayer is the heart's devoted turning to God to drive away evil and obtain what is good. Contemplation is when the mind is in some sort lifted to God and held above itself, so that it tastes the joys of everlasting sweetness.

Then he adds:

> Reading seeks for sweetness of a blessed life, meditation perceives it, prayer asks for it, contemplation tastes it. Reading, as it were, puts food whole into the mouth, meditation chews it and breaks it up, prayer extracts its flavour, contemplation is the sweetness itself which gladdens and refreshes.[26]

Then he further elaborates upon these four stages of becoming a person dedicated to the living Word. We struggle to overcome obstacles, namely "unavoidable necessity, the good works of the active life, human frailty and worldly follies" that would keep us from being the true contemplative.[27]

By the twelfth century there was also a polemical intent in this elaborated form of Bible reading. As Arnould of Boheries comments, "They should not seek knowledge *(scientia)* so much as wisdom *(sapientia)*."[28] Or as Bernard of Clairvaux expressed it, "To expound these words I need to steep my heart in them rather than to study them." It was the rise of scholasticism, as epitomized in the style of Abelard, that caused Bernard to warn against excessive speculation in theology and in the disputative use of the Scriptures. For contemplatives like Bernard, reading became much more of an ascetic than aesthetic experience, one that aroused love and ardor for Christ rather than merely arousing the senses of the natural man.

Hugh of St. Victor points out in his treatise on Bible reading, the *Didascalion,* that the privileged capacity of appropriate reading of the Scripture is to elicit this kind of spiritual response from the reader, as it is there alone that not only the words but also the events and things related have meaning, in expressing the acts of God in history.[29]

Over some sixteen centuries *lectio divina* has proved itself capable of transforming the reader in a remarkably long-lasting and institutionalized tradition. All can benefit, beginner and advanced, so that Bernard observed, "In the ocean of this sacred reading the lamb can paddle and the elephant swims."[30]

The Reformed Shift to the Grammatical and the Spirit-Guided Reading

In the late Middle Ages the increasing impact of textual reading within the universities led to a focus on *grammatical interpretation.* John Wyclif enunciated that scriptural interpretation could only proceed towards the truth if the logic and structure of the Bible itself formed the basic principles of its interpretation, that no mere exercise of *lectio divina* or recitation of authorities could substitute. Grammar then came to hold a larger implication in reading as the reader's intention came to hold a larger implication in reading, for the reader's intention must be to let Scripture interpret itself. In *The Truth of Sacred Scripture,* Wyclif argues that "a Christian ought to speak the word of Scripture under the authority of Scripture, according to the form of Scripture just as Scripture itself declares."[31] A response to the inner voice of Scripture is required of the reader.

This response to spiritual understanding was developed in medieval hermeneutics in the fourfold meaning that is recited in the following Latin verse:

Littera gesta docet; quid credas allegoria.

Moralis quid aga, sed quid speres, anagoge.

The literal sense or letter is speaking of the facts, deeds or events. The allegorical sense speaks of what is to be believed (applying it to the life of the church). The moral or tropological sense speaks of the meaning of the text for the life of the individual Christian in distinction from the ecclesiastical or allegorical sense. The anagogical deals with both the mystical life of the individual Christian and the eschatological events of the kingdom of God. In spite of this elaboration, the greatest medieval exegete in the thirteenth century, the Franciscan Nicholas of Lyra, a professor in Paris, was criticized later by Luther as having leaned too heavily upon the Jewish exegesis of Rashi in his interpretation of the Psalms. How does one break through the veil of "the letter" to find the "spiritual meaning" of the text, he asked?

This was what troubled Martin Luther. As Thomas Aquinas had done, Nicholas of Lyra posited a double literal meaning of the text—the first as the human author intended and the second as the divine author intended.[32] Luther heightened the second literal meaning by his christological focus, entitling his lectures on the Psalms, "Preface of Jesus Christ to the Psalter of David." In his second series of lectures on the Psalter after 1519 (the first course was in 1513-1515), Luther demanded that the anagogical should be ignored and that the christological emphasis of interpretation should be viewed as "literal" interpretation. Allegory should also be abolished, except as the metaphorical language used in the text itself. Indeed, in his later commentary on Genesis, he argued that any allegorical interpretation should be based on the historical and literal meaning of the text.

Along with the literal interpretation of the text, Luther now emphasized the overwhelming importance of the tropological, or as he called it, the "primary sense" of Scripture, quoting from Romans 15:4: "Whatever was written, was written for our instruction," that is, the moral instruction of our souls. It signifies the Christian's story within the story of the gospel. "Dying and rising with Christ" becomes the vital aim of the Bible reader. In his comments on Psalm 98:4, as our colleague Klaus Bockmuehl used to point out, he actually draws his own allegory. The two sorts of instruments the ancient Israelites blew, he argued, were the horn for occasions of suffering and affliction on the one hand, and the trumpet for festive occasions on the other.[33] These reflect upon the two kinds of preaching, of Law and Gospel respectively, so that dying under law we might live again under the Gospel. Hence the fourfold medieval framework of Bible reading was reduced by Luther to the twofold meaning of Scripture, the literal and the tropological or spiritual. This means that at least half of the action of interpretation and personal assimilation of Scripture reflects upon the work of God's Spirit within the mind and heart of the reader.

Unlike much modern biblical criticism, Luther was unwilling to make the sharp distinction between what the text meant to the author and what it now means to the reader. He expected the Word to be inexhaustible in its possibilities of liberating the reader within his own time frame and speaking therefore to every historical context. Rather than the emphasis upon the historical-critical methodology so prevalent today, he focused upon the moral requirements of the Bible reader. First, there was the need of humility. As he observed:

Scripture is not in our power nor in the ability of the mind. Therefore in its study we must in no way rely on our own understanding (that is, our intellectual powers) but we must become humble and pray that He may bring that understanding to us, since it is not given except to the humble. There are many who speculate sharply, but to no avail. Fear of the Lord is key to the understanding of Scripture, and the more fear of God there is, the more understanding.[34]

Secondly, Luther speaks of the need for congeniality with the text of Scripture, not as a matter of intellect, but of spirituality. "No one," he argues, "understands another in spiritual writings unless he savors and possesses the same spirit."[35] This law of correspondence he sees is also associated with two further aspects: affection and practice. By affection he means the ability and desire to feel inwardly what he reads outwardly, so that he conforms his heart to accept what is being communicated. It is the Spirit that so actualizes the whole being of the reader that the message received is put also into practice.

Thirdly, what one has understood as words now needs to be put into practice. As Luther also observed:

Works produce more understanding than words. He who does not put Scripture to the test in life and morals, very quickly misuses Scripture; he falls into error because he then measures Scripture by what he knows by himself. However, it is the works and practice which expound and understand the Scriptures.[36]

Fourthly, Luther sees interpretation and understanding of Scripture as open-ended. It has infinite meaning, and until the life to come it will have unlimited possibilities of revelation for the Bible reader. Luther therefore was very open to other possible interpretations, seeing the importance of the communion of the saints in Bible reading. Rather than believing he was giving exact tools for exegesis, Luther leaves open in his sermons alternate interpretations of the passage being interpreted.

The tendency of Reformed faith, whether Lutheran or Calvinist, was to favor preaching as the primary vehicle for the reading of the Scriptures, to the detriment often of the home Bible reader. This led initially to a rapid reform of doctrine that did not represent a reform of life for the ordinary church-goer. The Pietists saw a great need for reform to be taken further into the homes of the common people.

In his *Pia Desideria,* Philipp Spener says that "more is needed than simply the preaching of the Word."[37] Reading privately should also be encouraged. So he urges the establishment of informal Bible classes that permit those present to express their own understanding of the passage being considered. The ordained priesthood is ineffective in its ministry without encouraging the universal priesthood of all believers to be operative also. And this is most effective when there are home Bible groups that share together in Bible studies as families and friends.[38]

Later August Hermann Francke gave a short course of instruction on how Holy Scripture ought to be read for one's true edification. He listed eight points: read singlemindedly; let such reading be from purity of heart; approach God's Word reverently; read it prayerfully; meditate upon it leisurely; conclude the reading with prayer; read it in light of the cross; read also as having risen with Christ so that one's understanding is spiritually enlightened.[39] Francke pointed out that the scribes and Pharisees also read the Scriptures, so seek out any false motive for reading them, such as pride in appearing knowledgable and learned, self-glory, etc.

Puritanism has been rightly called a Bible movement. Some like John Owen laid stress upon the interpretation of Scripture as being church-related and taught by competent preachers. But others like John Rogers laid more stress upon personal Bible reading in the context of private meditation. Without constant reading of the Scriptures, observes Rogers, the Christian is liable to find his Christian life handicapped, for they are "profitable to teach, convince, to correct and instruct in righteousness."[40]

In his *Christian Directory* Richard Baxter exhorts, "Read and meditate on the Holy Scriptures much in private, and then you will be better able to understand what is preached on it in public, and to try the doctrine, whether it be of God."[41] This orientation to Bible reading as the focal importance of preaching explains Baxter's further injunction that deals with Bible hearing more than reading: "Live under the most convincing, lively, serious preacher that you possibly can." Then he adds some instructions about being a Bible reader: "Read it not as a common book, with a common or irreverent heart, but in the dread and love of God the author."[42] The Puritans taught that the Scriptures should be read reverently and humbly, with a teachable and obedient spirit. However, the Puritan preachers focused on the public interpretation of Scripture, which seems for them to hold more central importance than home and personal Bible reading.

The rise of deism and rationalism in the eighteenth century saw biblical criticism as no more than what is done with the text of any other literature. Against such a tendency Karl Barth observed:

> The Bible gives to every man and every era such answers to their questions as they deserve. We will always find in it as much as we seek and no more; high and divine content if it is high and divine content that we seek; transitory and "historical" content if it is transitory and "historical" content that we seek. The question: "What is within the Bible?" has a mortifying way of converting itself into the opposing question, "Well, what are you looking for, and who are you who made bold to look?" . . . The man who is looking for history or for stories will be glad after a little to turn from the Bible to the morning paper or to other books. . . . It is not the right human thoughts about God which form the content of the Bible, but the right divine thoughts about men. The Bible tells us not how we should talk with God but what he says to us.[43]

Just so! The whole scholarly debate over biblical hermeneutics has ultimately to face this issue: Is it scholarship or godliness that is the aim of the Bible reader? Is it directed to self-glorification or to the glory of the God who made it all possible?

Toward a Renewed Spirituality of Bible Reading
Following the Enlightenment the infallibility of the historical-critical method

of interpretation has been affirmed. As Benjamin Jowett, then Regius Professor at Oxford, affirmed in 1859: "Scripture has one meaning, the meaning which it had in the mind of the Prophet or Evangelist who first uttered or wrote, to the hearers who first received it."[44] So Scripture could be interpreted like any other book, and all venerated traditions should be brushed off. "The true use of interpretation is to get rid of interpretation and leave us alone in the company of the author."[45]

But Jowett did not foresee the great difficulties there would be in doing this, nor indeed have many subsequent exegetes realized the simple recognition that the process of technical interpretation is not the same as "Bible reading." The latter is more comprehensive than simply eliciting the plain meaning of the text, or indeed of attempting to reach back to the meaning as intended by the original author. The fourfold levels of interpretation that were recognized traditionally in medieval exegesis were flattened and reduced to two by Luther: the historical-literal and the spiritual. Now there is merely one level, the historical-critical. This makes an absolute (indeed an idol) out of one approach to the study of God's word, which is clearly wrong.

This is where German scholars such as Adolf Schlatter and Peter Stuhlmacher still struggle. Schlatter found his faith, his scholarship and his teaching quite inseparable. Using biblical criticism while maintaining his commitment to Christ created for him his "misery in relation to the Bible," in faithfulness to both personal faith in Christ and his Word, yet faithful also to biblical scholarship.[46]

Following him in a later generation at Tübingen, Peter Stuhlmacher faces some of the same misery in calling for a "hermeneutic of acceptance of the biblical texts." By this phrase he expresses his intent to retain the historical-critical method as the only "scientifically justified procedure." At the same time, he recognizes the church and its need to uphold the faith in service to biblical superiority as the source of truth. So he serves simultaneously the canons of modern judgment and of biblical authority. It remains therefore a theological mediation that will serve neither the secular world of scholarship nor the biblical realm of the faithful.[47]

In the face of this contemporary tension we are led to recite the words of the apostle: "The letter kills but the Spirit makes alive" (2 Cor 3:6). Is this to be interpreted, following Augustine, by distinguishing the law (that demands from the sinner what he is powerless to give) from the Spirit (that makes alive because of the grace given the gospel)? Or could it be interpreted that the "letter" is that storybook level of biblical text that is narrative whereas the Spirit is that deeper theological meaning that Luther and before him the medieval church recognized as a deep series of spiritual interpretations?

The modern exegete accepts in the text only what the author intended it to mean, in a far more radical way than medieval exegetes ever conceived of doing. It is almost as if the modern exegete actually knows better than the original author ever knew what he was writing or saying. Perhaps the medieval writer held a far more balanced perspective than we give credit today in seeing the Scriptures as containing both "letter" and "spirit." David Steinmetz thus advocates boldly that "the medieval theory of levels of meaning in the biblical text, with all its undoubted defects, flourished because it is true, while the modern theory of a single meaning, with all its demonstrable virtues, is false."[48]

From a similar perspective our colleague Bruce Waltke advocates that same return to "levels" of understanding. This he does selectively, rather than exhaustively, as indeed any modern reader can only do.[49] Such patristic and medieval interpretation might fairly be summed up in the words: "Beginning with Moses and all the Prophets, Jesus interpreted to them in all the Scriptures the things concerning himself" (Lk 24:27). It is a form of reading that sees the mystery of Christ as extending into the church and into the life of all Christians on earth as well as the life which is to be fulfilled in heaven. This is not so much a hermeneutic of logic and technique as of faith and its fulfillment in Christ. Such an approach is expressive of the attempts we make to live by the gospel, living by what we read as Bible readers. This implies far more than simply seeking a clear interpretation of the text. Modern biblical criticism seeks clarity of meaning and accuracy of interpretation regarding the author's original intention. Yet even the literal sense may have levels of meaning, since God's dealings with us human beings are manifold and mysterious indeed.

The mistake of so much modern biblical criticism seems to be fivefold: (1) too much professional domination over the lay reader of the Bible; (2) restricting Bible reading to merely interpreting the text; (3) focusing on the literary genres instead of applying them to personal living; (4) often ignoring the fact that great literature demands great readers, certainly those devout in godliness; and (5) the absence of a culture of Bible readers such as existed in the past.

Let me amplify upon these issues. First, it is an obvious social reality that lay reading of the Bible is dominated by professionalized exegesis and hermeneutics. How many young seminary students have had their prayer life and devotional attitudes toward Bible reading destroyed by professionalized instruction! How often have lay Christians heard attacks against the authority of Scripture by scholars given full freedom to speculate academically! Somewhat sarcastically, Jacques Ellul has commented that "hermeneutics is the business of interpreting revelation without revelation."[50] Christian exegetical labor should be seen as a vital spiritual activity. Did not Jesus himself condemn the scribes and the Pharisees? "You are in error because you do not know the Scriptures or the power of God" (Mt 23:29). The Bible is not properly understood without attentiveness to the Word of God by the Spirit of God.

It is the posture described so challengingly by our former colleague, Klaus Bockmuehl, in his last book, *Listening to the God Who Speaks*. The whole Bible, he observes, is a record of God's speaking to his people.[51] As we listen obediently to God, we will seek relentlessly to prevent professionalism from effacing true biblical convictions that concern our life as believing Christians. Professionalism is rooted more deeply in theory than practice, in abstract knowledge rather than personal behavior. We need scholarly work, but it should be oriented pastorally, for the well-being of the church, rather than professionally, concerned with what the academy might think. The true goal of Christian scholarship should be to affirm rather than to question, to be witness to the truth rather than to be a mere bystander, and to strengthen what is normative of Christian living rather than to speculate peripherally. All this is to affirm that the professional guild of biblical scholarship has to foster the nurture of Christian living rather than be absorbed in "academic gains" for their own sake.

Secondly, in recent decades much energy has been expended upon discussing the nature of biblical authority, the issue of inerrancy, the question of the inspiration of Scripture and the niceties of hermeneutics, that the actual cultivation of Bible reading has been largely overlooked. What is also overlooked is that Bible reading is much more comprehensive of the whole living of the Christian life than even the interpretation of biblical scholarship. Why do I read the Bible? Is it not because I am a Christian, desirous daily to know God more personally? Is it possible for me to progress and move forward without the certainty of living the Word of God? And as a Christian, how can I know the Scriptures without constant prayerful meditation? Just as the apostles devoted themselves to prayer and the ministry of the word (Acts 6:4), so we need to resonate to the truths and atmosphere of Scripture in daily walk. Instead, modern Scripture scholarship often treats its subject with a familiarity and clinical curiosity that is inconsistent with the character of biblical faith. It is good, then, to reflect on what it means to be like the meditator in Psalm 119, a Torah person so absorbed in God's Word that all emotions, attitudes and circumstances of life are centered wholly upon the presence of God and his Word in one's daily life. As Dietrich Bonhoeffer wrote in a letter to Karl Barth in 1935: "The kind of questions serious young theologians put to us are: 'How can I learn to pray? How can I learn to read the Bible?' Either we help them do this, or we cannot help them at all. Nothing of this can be taken for granted."[52] But we still take for granted that we are Bible readers. This is, in fact, far more difficult in our secular society than we admit. This reading challenges us to a greater transformation of the inner life than we may be willing to face.

Thirdly, modern biblical scholarship has given much attention to the literary genres of Scripture. This is introduced helpfully in Gordon Fee and Douglas Stuart's popular book, *How to Read the Bible for All Its Worth.* "We start our discussion of the various biblical genres," they say, "with the epistles."[53] This is a genre perhaps closest to our own mindset, so it is wise to start with it and then proceed to study the different kinds of narrative in the Old Testament. Then examine the gospel parables, recognizing their unique hermeneutical task, namely that when they were spoken they seldom ever needed to be interpreted! Wisdom literature, the Psalms, the Prophets, the book of Revelation—each has its distinctive genre that needs literary understanding in order to distinguish the novel from the poem. This approach helps us to elucidate the differing genres of Scripture in an intelligent way. Then deeper reflection may help us relate these genres to the emotional range of personal experiences we share as well as the temptations and differing stages of our spiritual growth.

Historically, meditation on the Psalms has brought about renewal of the biblical life. It was so for Martin Luther. Dietrich Bonhoeffer was renewed by meditation on Psalm 119. Perhaps dwelling each day with a verse of Psalm 119, and each week with one of the twenty-two stanzas of this psalm that celebrates and induces meditation upon the range and fullness of God's Word, will in half a year introduce the Bible reader to the spirit and cadence of Bible meditation.[54] Then reading the other psalms will lead us to recognize that the full range of all our emotions are expressed before God, as we move from lament to praise and thanksgiving, then on to repose and deeper trust. The devout heart has thus been given speech so that it no longer need remain silent in misunderstanding and loneliness. By the wide range of experiences of David's own life a whole range of emotions are expressed before God, in which we are invited to share.

In recent scholarship much attention has been directed to the way that narrative, as personal storytelling, helps to shape self-understanding and nurture morality. It is a welcome shift from the generalized theories of ethicists to viewing ethics within the context of individual narratives. The Bible is filled with such personal stories. This is a genre that fits well into the personal needs of the Bible reader. The moral response required of the one who reads the gospel parables is also an engagement in which the Bible reader has to relate and make response. Bible reading in its appropriate forms of response to each type of genre has life-giving qualities that the Spirit of God quickens within the reader. The Spirit of God who inspired the scriptural writers to compose their works is the same Spirit who inspires the reader to respond to what they have written. It is salutatory to remember, as C. S. Lewis pointed out, that "those who read the Bible as literature do not read the Bible. . . . Unless the religious claims of the Bible are again acknowledged, its literary claims will, I think, be given only 'mouth honour' and that decreasingly."[55]

Fourthly, it is a well-known axiom that great literature requires great readers. Mortimer Adler in his refreshing work *How to Read a Book* identifies the steps needed to read well, and most importantly, to cultivate our minds to be free and to live happily. A mind trained to think clearly is also a mind disciplined to think freely. Adler sees several essential steps: to understand the author's words (lexical study); to find and appreciate the author's arguments (logical study); and to see the problems that need to be solved.[56] And that is only the beginning. How much more is required of the Bible reader! As the apostle puts it, "These are written that you may believe that Jesus is the Christ, the Son of God, and that by believing you may have life in his name" (Jn 20:31). Becoming a Bible reader involves becoming a Christian, in all the depth and fullness of what the apostle speaks of as being "in Christ." All the virtues and the graces of being a Christian are necessary to grow as a reader of the Word of God. If classical literature was promoted for exemplary reading, how much more is the reading of the Scriptures a moral and personal challenge for the transformation of our values, desires and way of life!

Finally we have to ask, Do we have a culture of Bible reading like the *lectio divina* in the Middle Ages or of exemplary reading as in the early church? Clearly we have neither. While Bible study groups and membership in church fellowships are valuable assets to spiritual growth, such tend to be more informative than life-changing. Protestant preachers, such as Charles Simeon, have sometimes exhibited a rare zeal for ordering all their thought and life around the Scriptures. But it is rare to think of lay Bible readers wholly oriented and motivated by the Word of God. As a lifelong student of Scripture, Simeon could affirm:

> There is nothing in the whole universe to be compared with the Scriptures of truth. . . . nothing that will so enrich the mind, nothing that will so benefit the soul. To treasure them up in our minds should be our daily and most delightful employment. Not a day should pass without adding to their blessed store, and not only in memory and mind, but in heart and soul.[57]

To exercise such deep involvement with prayer and Bible reading, Simeon rose each morning at four o'clock and followed a rigorous regimen of study. But such exemplars are rare, and where they do exist they provide no practical framework for their own congregations or other Bible readers to imitate.

In our day the church needs a renewal and reform that will play a role as vital as the rise of monasticism was during the fall of the Roman Empire or as the Protestant Reformation was in ushering in the modern world. What role will Bible reading play in the motivation of Christian reform now?

Firstly, it requires a renewed awareness of the transcendent power of the revelation of God to a secular world in which God appears to have been eclipsed. Erich Auerbach, in his brilliant study *Mimesis: The Representation of Reality in Western Literature,* notes that "the text of the biblical narrative . . . is so greatly in need of interpretation on the basis of its own content, its claim to absolute authority forces it still further in the same direction."[58] This was comparatively easy in the Middle Ages. But the awakening of the modern critical spirit has made it much more difficult in modern times. What is needed now is the sharpening of the divide between biblical narrative and that of secular, indeed, classical literature. The biblical claim to universal history, the insistent demand made of the reader to the sovereign claim of a single God who guides and promises, and the moral response required of the reader to the claims of divine authorship are wholly contrasted with the elements in secular or classical authorship. The unique world of the Bible needs reaffirmation in our times.

How? we may ask. As we affirm the reality of God in our lives, we are already being awakened to the need of conversion. The power of holy Scripture lies in that when we open ourselves to listen to it, it commands us to repent, to be turned around and to live antithetically to where we have gravitated naturally. As Karl Barth expressed it, conversion is like awakening out of sleep and arising to follow God rather than accepting the natural inclination of our senses. Confronted by the Scriptures, we also find that conversion embraces the whole person, both inwardly and outwardly. It implies engagement with the Word of God in our hearts, minds and will, both privately and publicly. Encounter with Scripture also demands that we pursue always a holy life. It is a life movement that compels and impels us, emotionally, intellectually and volitionally. No other literature can ever have the same holistic and transforming power and authority.

With conversion the Word of God creates personal freedom for us. Scripture is not "koranic" or legalistic, engaging us in some automatic process of religious sentiment. The Spirit of God, who inspired it, also illumines it. We need to wrestle with the Word in every way possible, with exegesis, with criticism or analysis, and with all the latest insights of further scholarship. Yet we must still read it simply in devotional acceptance of its message to our hearts, as given of God. All of these approaches must be directed to the glory of God if the Word would set us free. As Ellul has warned us:

> Criticism is not to become an apologetic machine, which brings no true glory to God, but simply presents an uninteresting theory of God and shows no freedom. Criticism in true freedom in Christ leads to a better exposition of God's revelation, i.e., his glory and to more fitting worship of the Lord.[59]

Such freedom in the text of Scripture never destroys the faith of others because it will be always expressive of love, thus bringing the love of God into the lives of others. If we do otherwise, then our exegetical motives are wrong and destructive. This is the crux. It is because I am free in Christ that I enjoy and share the Word of God with others, so that I give glory to God in response to his Word and share love with others as I live by his Word.

To conversion and personal freedom we add that the Word of God enriches our humanity. As von Balthasar has observed:

Man is the being created as the hearer of the Word, and only in responding to the Word arises to his full dignity. He was conceived in the mind
of God as the partner in dialogue. . . . His inmost being is readiness,
attentiveness, perceptiveness, willingness to surrender to what is greater
than he, to let the deeper truth prevail, to lay down his arms at the feet
of enduring love.[60]

Yet von Balthasar further observes that Protestantism with its sense of divine revelation has taken a strong stance in interpreting the Word, whereas Roman Catholicism has fallen short of a like hearing of it. Both traditions therefore need a reversal of posture: the Protestant, to be more unreservedly open to receive the Word as Mary did, in the spirit of contemplation; the Catholic, to pay loyal attention to the content of the Word in deeper understanding.[61] We need to deepen both the capacity and the content of the contemplative posture before God's Word as we realize that our personal lives remain ad-dictive and unfree, emotionally and cognitively, without being contemplatives of the Word. It is in contemplation before the Word that we are turned toward the truth of our existence, not our own, but God's truth, so that we may come to live more fully, in faith and obedience, by this truth. This act of contem-plation before the Word is again an act of the whole person, not just as a scholar or even as a Bible inquirer, but wholly so.

The "act of Bible reading," then, is far more than learning techniques and becoming knowledgable in exegesis and hermeneutics. It opens us to being inspired intelligently and affectively in the way of truth.[62] The Word of God is the means of growth in Christian living, opening us up to new situations of faith, as a "lamp unto our feet and a light unto our way." Since its focus is on Christ, we get to know him intimately as we live by his Word. It teaches us to experience and know what is Christian discipleship, with concrete teach-ing that we can apply practically to our lives. It presents us with the principles and norms for "living the gospel." Moreover, it constantly reminds us of the initiatives and acts of God so that we develop more responsively before God. In "proclamation" we are called upon to constantly restate its message in our contemporary world. Likewise, the Word of God upholds divine community, seeing the church as the perennial miracle of continuity, of God continuously active in the midst of his people.

Notes

Chapter 2: Canon as Context for Interpretation/Dyck

[1]For the view that the New Testament writers used the Old Testament in a way that was both apologetic and moralistic, see L. Kugel and Rowan A. Greer, *Early Biblical Interpretation,* Library of Early Christianity (Philadelphia: Westminster Press, 1986), pp. 126-36. A more substantial treatment can be found in Hans von Campenhausen, *The Formation of the Christian Bible,* trans. J. A. Baker (Philadelphia: Fortress, 1972).

[2]Irenaeus was the first to use the terms *Old Testament* and *New Testament* to define the collections *as collections (Against Heresies* 4.15.2).

[3]The older histories of interpretation such as F. W. Farrar, *History of Interpretation* (New York: Dutton, 1886), and Milton S. Terry, *Biblical Interpretation: A Treatise on the Interpretation of the Old and New Testaments,* rev. ed. (New York: Easton and Maines, 1890), continue to be useful, even if somewhat unfairly prejudiced against certain earlier types of interpretation. More recent are Robert M. Grant and David Tracey, *A Short History of Interpretation,* 2nd ed. (Philadelphia: Fortress, 1984), and *The Cambridge History of the Bible,* 3 vols. (Cambridge: Cambridge University Press, 1963-1970). Useful collections containing primary documentation can be found in Joseph W. Trigg, *Biblical Interpretation* (Willmington, Del.: Michael Glazier, 1988), and Karlfried Froehlich, ed. and trans., *Biblical Interpretation in the Early Church* (Philadelphia: Fortress, 1984).

[4]C. H. Dodd, *According to the Scriptures: The Sub-structure of New Testament Theology* (London: Nisbett, 1952), and *The Apostolic Preaching and Its Development* (reprint ed. London: Hodder & Stoughton, 1963).

[5]Jean Cardinal Danielou, *From Shadows to Reality: Studies in the Biblical Typology of the Fathers,* trans. Dom Wulstan Hibberd (London: Burns and Oates, 1960).

[6]Trigg, *Biblical Interpretation,* pp. 19-20.

[7]R. T. France, *Jesus and the Old Testament* (London: Tyndale, 1971).

[8]Jaroslav Pelikan, *Luther the Expositor: Introduction to the Reformer's Exegetical Writings* (St. Louis: Concordia, 1959).

[9]Of the many useful histories of the movement, see especially James Barr, *Old and New in Interpretation* (London: SCM Press, 1966), and Brevard S. Childs, *Biblical Theology in Crisis* (Philadelphia: Westminster Press, 1970).

[10]Walter Kaiser's otherwise challenging work falters at this point. See especially his reading of Matthew's use of Hosea 11:1 in *The Uses of the Old Testament in the New* (Chicago: Moody Press, 1985).

[11]For a review of Childs, Sanders and others see my Ph.D. dissertation, "Canon and Interpretation: Recent Canonical Approaches and the Book of Jonah," McGill University, 1987.

[12]James Barr is probably the most vocal in this regard. See his *Old and New in Interpretation* (London: SCM Press, 1966), and *The Bible in the Modern World* (London: SCM Press, 1973).

[13]James A. Sanders, "Hermeneutics," in *The Interpreter's Dictionary of the Bible: Supplementary Volume,* ed. Keith Crim (Nashville: Abingdon, 1976), p. 404.

[14]This account is easily reconstructed from the biblical record itself. For a fuller history, see John Bright, *A History of Israel,* 3rd ed. (Philadelphia: Westminster, 1981), pp. 276-78.

[15]John Oswalt, *Isaiah 1—39,* New International Commentary on the Old Testament (Grand Rapids, Mich.: Eerdmans, 1986).

[16]Morton Coggin, *Imperialism and Religion,* Society of Biblical Literature Monograph Series 19 (Missoula, Mont.: Scholars Press, 1974).

[17]Bruce K. Waltke and M. O'Connor, *An Introduction to Biblical Hebrew Syntax* (Winona Lake, Ind.: Eisenbrauns, 1990), p. 241.

[18]Otto Kaiser, *Isaiah 1-12,* 2nd ed. trans. John Bowden, Old Testament Library (Philadelphia: Westminster Press, 1983), pp. 154-55.

[19]The fact that *bᵉṯûlâh* seems to require further qualification suggests that this term is equally ambiguous. See G. J. Wenham, "Betula: A Girl of Marriageable Age," *Vetus Testamentum* 22 (1972): 335-48.

[20]So also H. M. Wolf, "A Solution to the Immanuel Prophecy in Isaiah 7:14—8:22," *Journal of Biblical Literature* 91 (1972): 449-56. J. Alec Motyer's counterargument, that not only are the two distinct children but the second releases the former (Immanuel) from the here and now—that he is projected into the indefinite hereafter—is not at all compelling *(The Prophecy of Isaiah: An Introduction and Commentary* [Downers Grove, Ill.: InterVarsity Press, 1993], pp. 90-91).

[21]Bright, *History of Israel,* p. 270.

[22]I find it astonishing that Motyer, in his recent commentary *(Prophecy of Isaiah,* p. 101), never even considers and therefore never provides argument against this position. He does admit that this has become Assyrian territory but then argues that the

conquest is not a real conquest at all. The word is a mere metaphor for a "spreading peace, and in its fulfilment . . . the work of evangelism."

[23]Edwin P. Theile, *The Mysterious Numbers of the Hebrew Kings,* rev. ed. (Grand Rapids, Mich.: Zondervan, 1983), pp. 163-76.

[24]See the description in Waltke and O'Connor, *Introduction to Biblical Hebrew Syntax,* p. 490. Note, however, against my conclusion, that Waltke does consider the text in question to be a special example of a prophetic perfect.

[25]See Brevard S. Childs, "Prophecy and Fulfilment: A Study in Contemporary Hermeneutics," *Interpretation* 12 (1958): 260-71.

Chapter 3: Theology & Bible Reading/Packer

[1]J. I. Packer, foreword to Bruce Milne, *Know the Truth* (Leicester, U.K.; Downers Grove, Ill.: Inter-Varsity Press, 1982).

[2]John Wenham, "Personally Speaking," *Themelios* 18, no. 1 (1992): 35. In a similar vein John Stott stated, "When I was myself an undergraduate at Cambridge during World War II, the Divinity School was entirely liberal in its orientation. . . . If anybody was rash enough to read for the Theology tripos, and managed to survive, it was regarded as a miracle" (*Christian Arena* 45 [1992]: 27).

[3]Mark Noll (*Between Faith and Criticism* [San Francisco: Harper, 1987]) tells the American side of the story. The British side has not yet been fully documented.

[4]Schaff translates the Apostles' Creed as follows:

I believe in GOD THE FATHER Almighty; Maker of heaven and earth.

And in JESUS CHRIST his only (begotten) Son our Lord; who was conceived by the Holy Ghost, born of the Virgin Mary; suffered under Pontius Pilate, was crucified, dead, and buried; he descended into hell [Hades, spirit world]; the third day he rose from the dead; he ascended into heaven; and sitteth at the right hand of God the Father Almighty; from thence he shall come to judge the quick and the dead.

I believe in the HOLY GHOST; the holy catholic Church; the communion of the saints; the forgiveness of sins; the resurrection of the body [flesh]; and the life everlasting. Amen. (Philip Schaff, *The Creeds of Christendom* [reprint, Grand Rapids, Mich.: 1990] 2.45)

[5]Alister McGrath, *Understanding Doctrine* (London: Hodder & Stoughton, 1990), p. 10.

[6]Ibid., p. 124.

[7]Ibid., p. 128.

[8]John Calvin, *Institutes of the Christian Religion,* trans. F. L. Battles (Philadelphia: Westminster Press, 1960), pp. 4-5.

Chapter 4: The Sociology of Knowledge & the Art of Suspicion/Gay

[1]Karl Marx, "The German Ideology," in *The Portable Karl Marx,* ed. Eugene Kamenka (New York: Viking/Penguin, 1983), p. 169.

[2]Karl Mannheim, *Ideology and Utopia: An Introduction to the Sociology of Knowledge* (London: Routledge and Kegan Paul, 1936).

[3]José Míguez Bonino, *Doing Theology in a Revolutionary Situation* (Philadelphia: Fortress, 1975), pp. 17-18.

[4]Letty Russell, "Introduction: Liberating the Word," in *Feminist Interpretation of the Bible,* ed. Letty M. Russell (Philadelphia: Westminster Press, 1985), p. 11.

[5]Rosemary Radford Ruether, "Feminist Interpretation: A Method of Correlation," in *Feminist Interpretation of the Bible,* ed. Letty M. Russell (Philadelphia: Westminster Press, 1985), p. 114.

[6]James Cone, *A Black Theology of Liberation,* 2nd ed. (Maryknoll, N.Y.: Orbis, 1986), p. 45.

[7]Ibid., p. vii.

[8]Elisabeth Schüssler Fiorenza, "The Will to Choose or to Reject: Continuing Our Critical Work," in *Feminist Interpretation of the Bible,* ed. Letty M. Russell (Philadelphia: Westminster Press, 1985), p. 132.

[9]Cone, *Black Theology of Liberation,* p. 9.

[10]Rosemary Radford Ruether, "Feminist Interpretation: A Method of Correlation," in *Feminist Interpretation of the Bible,* ed. Letty M. Russell (Philadelphia: Westminster Press, 1985), p. 121.

[11]Robert A. Nisbet, *Community and Power* (Oxford: Oxford University Press, 1962), p. 33.

[12]Peter Collier and David Horowitz, *Destructive Generation: Second Thoughts About the Sixties* (New York: Summit, 1989), p. 313.

[13]Peter Berger, *The Sacred Canopy: Elements of a Sociological Theory of Religion* (Garden City, N.Y.: Anchor, 1969), p. 181.

Chapter 5: Hermeneutics & the Postmodern Reaction Against "Truth"/Wilkinson

[1]Frank Kermode, *The Genesis of Secrecy: On the Interpretation of Narrative* (Cambridge, Mass.: Harvard University Press, 1979), p. vii.

[2]Ibid.

[3]Ibid., p. viii.

[4]Ibid., p. xi.

[5]Ibid.

[6]Richard Rorty, *Philosophy and the Mirror of Nature* (Princeton, N.J.: Princeton University Press, 1979), p. 316.

[7]Ibid., p. 318.

[8]Richard Rorty, *Consequences of Pragmatism* (Minneapolis: University of Minnesota Press, 1982), p. xviii.

[9]Martin Heidegger, *Being and Time,* trans. John Macquarrie and Edward Robinson (New York: Harper & Row, 1962), p. 58.

[10]Ibid., p. 193.

[11]Ibid., p. 195.

[12]Hans-Georg Gadamer, *Truth and Method* (New York: Seabury, 1975), p. 239.

[13]Ibid., p. 238.

[14]Ibid., p. 264.

[15]The concept is the source of the title of Anthony Thiselton's *The Two Horizons,* which comprehensively and appreciatively catalogs the implications of the thought of both Heidegger and Gadamer for biblical hermeneutics. Anthony Thiselton, *The Two Horizons: New Testament Hermeneutics and Philosophical Description* (Grand Rapids, Mich.: Eerdmans, 1980).

[16]Gadamer, *Truth and Method,* pp. 264-65.

[17]E. D. Hirsch, *Validity in Interpretation* (New Haven: Yale University Press, 1967), pp. 250-51.

[18]Jonathan Culler, *On Deconstruction* (Ithaca, N.Y.: Cornell University Press, 1982), p. 22.

[19]Jacques Derrida, *Writing and Difference,* trans. Alan Bass (Chicago: University of Chicago Press, 1978), p. 280.

[20]Jacques Derrida, *Of Grammatology,* trans. Gayatri Chakravorty Spivak (Baltimore: Johns Hopkins University Press, 1976), p. 50.

[21]There is, of course, a deep paradox in *saying* that *no* saying can have a particular meaning. If "true," it eliminates the possibility of saying (or meaning) anything at all and reduces one to silence. All the same, there is more than one instance of an avowed deconstructionist (including Derrida himself) arguing with very little playfulness *that he has been misunderstood.* See Ellis, *Against Deconstruction,* especially his discussion of a notorious argument between Derrida and John Searle. Says Ellis, "Derrida thus abandons this position [that the reader should not try to grasp the author's intent], just as others do, when he feels the need to replace a misstatement of his view with an adequate statement of it" (p. 14).

[22]Michel Foucault, "Truth and Power," in *Power/Knowledge: Selected Interviews and Other Writings, 1972-1977,* ed. Colin Gordon (New York: Pantheon, 1980), p. 133.

[23]Ibid., p. 123.

[24]Ibid.

[25]Frank Kermode, *The Genesis of Secrecy: On the Interpretation of Narrative* (Cambridge: Harvard University Press, 1979), p. 18.

[26]Michael E. Lodahl, "Jews and Christians in a Conflict of Interpretation," *Christian Scholar's Review* 19, no. 4 (1990): 334.

[27]José Míguez Bonino, *Doing Theology in a Revolutionary Situation* (Philadelphia: Fortress, 1975), pp. 88-89.

[28]Ibid., p. 91.

[29]Ibid.

[30]Peter Berger, *Pyramids of Sacrifice: Political Ethics and Social Change* (New York: Basic Books, 1974).

[31]The inclusive-language movement is the most successful aspect of the politically correct language movement—and it too is based on the premise that even our pronouns

perpetuate a power-driven picture of the world.

³²Thomas Kuhn, *The Structure of Scientific Revolutions* (Chicago: University of Chicago Press, 1962).

³³Rorty, *Consequences of Pragmatism,* p. xliii.

³⁴Ibid.

³⁵Ibid.

³⁶Roger Lundin, "Our Hermeneutical Inheritance," in Roger Lundin, Anthony Thiselton and Clarence Walhout, *The Responsibility of Hermeneutics* (Grand Rapids, Mich.: Eerdmans, 1985), p. 6.

³⁷Two works that spell out this line of argument at some length are Hirsch, *Validity in Interpretation,* which has an appendix directed specifically at Gadamer; and John M. Ellis, *Against Deconstruction* (Princeton, N.J.: Princeton University Press, 1989). Ellis takes on the much more radical deconstructive position exemplified by Derrida. Both Hirsch and Ellis argue strongly that as soon as one speaks or writes a word for the purpose of communication, one has an intention to be understood, an intention that *is* the "presence" that the postmodernist hermeneutic would like to deny.

³⁸James Olthuis, "A Cold and Comfortless Hermeneutic or a Warm and Trembling Hermeneutic: A Conversation with John D. Caputo," *Christian Scholar's Review* 19, no. 4 (1990): 345-62.

³⁹Ibid., p. 345.

⁴⁰Ibid., p. 346.

⁴¹That disagreement Olthuis refers to as the "Gadamer-Derrida encounter." It is summed up in a book (based on a discussion between the two thinkers in Paris in 1981) called *Dialogue and Deconstruction: The Gadamer-Derrida Encounter,* ed. Diane P. Michelfelder and Richard E. Palmer (New York: State University of New York Press, 1989).

⁴²Olthuis, "Cold and Comfortless," p. 351.

⁴³Ibid., p. 352.

⁴⁴Ibid.

⁴⁵Ibid.

⁴⁶Ibid., p. 353.

⁴⁷J. R. R. Tolkien, "On Fairy-Stories," in *Essays Presented to Charles Williams,* ed. C. S. Lewis (Grand Rapids, Mich.: Eerdmans, 1966), pp. 71-72.

⁴⁸Michael Polanyi, *Personal Knowledge: Towards a Post-critical Philosophy* (Chicago: University of Chicago Press, 1958), p. vii.

⁴⁹Ibid., p. viii.

⁵⁰Ibid., p. 104.

⁵¹Jerry Gill, "On Seeing Through a Glass, Darkly," *Christian Scholar's Review* 5, no. 3 (1976): 270.

⁵²Martin Heidegger, "Memorial Address," in *Discourse on Thinking,* trans. John Anderson and Hans Freund (New York: Harper & Row, 1966), p. 55. "Releasement" translates the German word *Gelassenheit,* which as the translators note "was used by

early German mystics (as Meister Eckhart) in the sense of letting the world go and giving oneself to God."

[53]Ibid., p. 46.

[54]Ibid., p. 50.

[55]Martin Heidegger, "Language," in *Poetry, Language, Thought,* trans. Albert Hofstadter (New York: Harper & Row, 1971), p. 209.

[56]Martin Heidegger, "The Origin of the Work of Art," in *Poetry, Language, Thought,* p. 53.

Chapter 6: Toward a Biblical Spirituality/Houston

[1]Robert K. Logan, *The Alphabet Effect: The Impact of the Phonetic Alphabet on Western Civilization* (New York: William Morrow, 1986), p. 81.

[2]See James M. Houston, *I Believe in the Creator* (London: Hodder & Stoughton, 1978).

[3]Lewis Mumford, *Technics and Human Development* (New York: Harcourt Brace Jovanovich, 1974), p. 96.

[4]Albert Camus, *The Rebel* (New York: Alfred A. Knopf, 1967), pp. 283-84.

[5]Philip Rhinelander, *Is Man Incomprehensible to Man?* (San Francisco: Freeman, 1974), p. 35.

[6]David Tracy, *The Anagogical Imagination: Christian Theology and the Culture of Pluralism* (New York: Crossroad, 1981), pp. 1-28.

[7]Helen Gardner, *The Business of Criticism* (London: Oxford University Press, 1959), pp. 3-24.

[8]Anthony Thiselton, *The Two Horizons* (Grand Rapids, Mich.: Eerdmans, 1980), pp. 15-16.

[9]Terence Hawkes, *Structuralism and Semiotics* (London: Methuen, 1977), pp. 156-60.

[10]Richard Palmer, "Postmodern Hermeneutics and the Act of Reading," *Notre Dame English Journal* 15, no. 3 (1983): 55-84.

[11]Paul Ricouer, *Hermeneutics and the Human Sciences: Essays on Language, Action and Interpretation,* ed. and trans. John B. Thompson (London: Cambridge University Press, 1981), p. 164.

[12]Palmer, "Postmodern Hermeneutics," pp. 62-69.

[13]A. J. Festugiere, *Antioche paienne et Christienne* (Paris: E. de Boccard, 1959), pp. 211-25.

[14]Henri-Irenee Marrou, *A History of Education in the Ancient World* (New York: Sheed and Ward, 1956), pp. 96-101, 217-26.

[15]See Peter R. L. Brown, "The Rise and Function of the Holy Man," in *Society and the Holy in Late Antiquity* (Berkeley: University of California Press, 1982), pp. 103-52.

[16]Werner Jaeger, *Early Christianity and Greek Paideia* (Cambridge, Mass.: Harvard University Press, 1993), p. 92.

[17]Quoted by Brown, "Rise and Function," p. 15.

[18]Robin Lane Fox, *Pagans and Christians* (London: Penguin, 1980), p. 304.

[19]Benedicta Ward, "Spiritual Direction in the Desert Fathers," *The Way* 24 (1984): 64-65.

[20]Quoted by Douglas Burton-Christie, *The Word in the Desert* (New York: Oxford University Press, 1993), p. 118.

[21]Ibid., p. 127.

[22]Ibid., pp. 261-91.

[23]*Origen,* trans. Rowan Greer (New York: Paulist, 1979), p. 32.

[24]Philip Rousseau, *Ascetics, Authority and the Church* (London: Oxford University Press, 1978), p. 70.

[25]Jean Leclerq, "Ways of Prayer and Contemplation," in *Christian Spirituality 1,* ed. Bernard McGinn and John Meyendorff (New York: Crossroad, 1985), pp. 415-26.

[26]*The Ladder of Monks: A Letter on the Contemplative Life and Twelve Meditations,* trans. Edmund Colledge (Kalamazoo, Mich.: Cistercian Publications, 1981), pp. 68-69.

[27]Ibid., p. 84.

[28]Quoted by Monica Sandor, "Lectio Divina and the Monastic Spirituality of Reading," *American Benedictine Review* 40, no. 1 (1989): 83-114, quote at p. 100.

[29]Ibid., p. 107.

[30]Ibid., p. 110.

[31]David Lyle Jeffrey, "John Wyclif and the Hermeneutics of Reader Response," *Interpretation* 39 (1985): 272-87, quote at p. 278.

[32]James Samuel Preus, *From Shadow to Promise* (Cambridge, Mass.: Harvard University Press, 1965), pp. 67-71.

[33]Klaus Bockmuehl, "The Hermeneutics of Luther," unpublished lecture notes.

[34]Ibid., p. 20.

[35]Ibid.

[36]Ibid., p. 21.

[37]Philip Jacob Spener, *Pia Desideria,* trans. Theodore G. Trappert (Philadelphia: Fortress, 1964), p. 87.

[38]Ibid., pp. 89-90.

[39]August Hermann Francke, *A Guide to the Reading and Study of the Holy Scriptures* (London: D. Jaques, 1813).

[40]On the Puritans' use of Scripture see John R. Knott, *The Sword and the Spirit: Puritan Responses to the Bible* (Chicago: University of Chicago Press, 1980).

[41]Richard Baxter, "The Christian Directory," in *The Practical Works,* ed. William Orme, (London: James Duncan, 1883), 4:265.

[42]Ibid.

[43]Karl Barth, *Church Dogmatics,* ed. Geoffrey Bromiley and Thomas Torrance (Edinburgh: T & T Clark, 1958), 4:564.

[44]Benjamin Jowett, "On the Interpretation of Scripture," in *Essays and Reviews* (London: Longman, Green and Roberts, 1861), p. 378.

LE READING

[45]Ibid., p. 3

[46]See Peter _____ ' _New Testament Stu_

[47]Gerhard _____ d," _Evangel-
ical Revie_

[48]David St_____ y Today_ 37
(1980): 27

[49]Bruce K. _____ unpublished
manuscri

[50]Quoted by _____ itics," _Inter-
pretation_

[51]Klaus Bo_____ ings, Colo.:
Helmers a

[52]Dietrich E_____ Cambridge,
Mass.: Co

[53]Gordon D_____ orth (Grand
Rapids, M

[54]See Bonho_____ :1-21.

[55]C. S. Lewi_____ offrey Bles,
1968), p. 6

[56]Mortimer _____ r, 1956), p.
235.

[57]Charles Si_____ (Portland,
Ore.: Mult

[58]Erich Aue_____ Literature
(Princeton

[59]Jacques Ellul, _The Ethics of Freedom,_ trans. Geoffrey Bromiley (Grand Rapids, Mich.: Eerdmans, 1976), p. 166.

[60]Hans Urs von Balthasar, _On Prayer,_ trans. A. V. Littledale (London: S.P.C.K., 1973), pp. 18-19.

[61]Ibid., pp. 23-26.

[62]For a simple, practical guide to contemporary Bible reading see George Martin, _Reading Scripture as the Word of God_ (Ann Arbor, Mich.: Servant, 1982).